The Secret to Creating and Sustaining
a Successful Business

The One Minute Entrepreneur™

Ken Blanchard
Don Hutson
and
Ethan Willis

CURRENCY  DOUBLEDAY

New York   London   Toronto   Sydney   Auckland

A CURRENCY BOOK
PUBLISHED BY DOUBLEDAY

Published in the United States by Doubleday, an imprint of The Doubleday Broadway
Publishing Group, a division of Random House, Inc., New York.
www.currencybooks.com

CURRENCY is a trademark of Random House, Inc., and DOUBLEDAY is a
registered trademark of Random House, Inc.

Library of Congress Cataloging-in-Publication Data
Blanchard, Kenneth H.
The One minute entrepreneur : the secret to creating and sustaining a successful business /
Ken Blanchard, Don Hutson, and Ethan Willis. — 1st ed.
p. cm.
1. New business enterprises. 2. Entrepreneurship. 3. Success in business.
I. Hutson, Don, 1945– II. Willis, Ethan. III. Title.

HD62.5.B56 2007
658.1'1—dc22

2007040540
ISBN: 978-0-385-52602-9

PRINTED IN THE UNITED STATES OF AMERICA

SPECIAL SALES
Currency Books are available at special discounts for bulk purchases for sales promotions
or premiums. Special editions, including personalized covers, excerpts of existing books,
and corporate imprints, can be created in large quantities for special needs. For more information, write to Special Markets, Currency Books, specialmarkets@randomhouse.com.

1 3 5 7 9 10 8 6 4 2

First Edition

Advance Praise for
THE ONE MINUTE ENTREPRENEUR

"I promise you will be a better person for absorbing the wisdom of this book. By the time you have read *The One Minute Entrepreneur,* you will know this wisdom was meant for you."

> **—Don M. Green, executive director, Napoleon Hill Foundation**

"*The One Minute Entrepreneur* is must reading for anyone who wants to improve their leadership skills. Great leaders are blessed by good followers, and this can only be accomplished by helping other people grow. This practical book will help in all aspects of your personal and professional life as an entrepreneur."

> **—Ron Glosser, president, Hershey Trust (retired)**

"*The One Minute Entrepreneur* is filled with gems of wisdom. Read it if you're serious about reinventing your life."

> **—Mark Sanborn, president, Sanborn and Associates, and author of *The Fred Factor***

"There is much said about stewardship in life and business; most of the time it's a reflection on money and material assets. However, the greatest stewardship is of influence. *The One Minute Entrepreneur* will teach you the importance of influence and inspire you to choose mentors wisely."

> **—Jim Amos, chairman emeritus, UPS**

"We each have a lot more to learn and a lot more to teach. *The One Minute Entrepreneur* will help you do both."

> **—R. Brad Martin, chairman of the board, Saks Incorporated**

"This book may be small in appearance, but it is big on ideas and ways to take advantage of other people's wisdom. It is a quick read, but the ideas will stay with you for a lifetime."

> **—Paul J. Meyer, founder of Success Motivation Institute and *New York Times* bestselling author**

"Don Hutson and Ken Blanchard have captured the essence of an entrepreneur's influence. Many great entrepreneurs have impacted my life. It has been my honor and pleasure to pass this on. What a joy and blessing it is to see others benefit and grow from an idea or experience you pick up along the way."

> **—Howard Putnam, former CEO, Southwest Airlines; speaker, and author of *The Winds of Turbulence***

"*The One Minute Entrepreneur* is an enjoyable read that provides a unique learning experience. Don Hutson and Ken Blanchard have done a beautiful job of teaching the concept of entrepreneurship and at the same time honoring the contributions of one of the heroes of the professional speaking field."

> **—Zig Ziglar, author and motivational teacher**

The One Minute Entrepreneur™

Dedication

This book is dedicated to the thousands of entrepreneurs who have braved countless obstacles and hung in through good times and bad to create successful companies. These firms are the backbone of the free-enterprise system.

We also dedicate this book to two such pioneers in particular: Charlie "Tremendous" Jones and Sheldon Bowles.

Tremendous Jones has been a mentor to both of us for years. From the quality, one-on-one time he has given to thousands, to his extraordinary speeches to millions, we have seen him impact the world—ours included—one life at a time. His love of books—resulting in the founding of his own entrepreneurial venture, Executive Books, some four decades ago—has touched people around the world. His personal works, coupled with his encouragement of reading, have helped countless people improve their lives and achieve their dreams. His unbridled passion for business has inspired many entrepreneurs in their quest to build great companies. This mountain of a man stands so tall in his spiritual walk that it is impossible not to be inspired by his faith. His enthusiasm is boundless, his friendships deep, and his leadership profound.

Sheldon Bowles has had a tremendous impact on the thinking and business lives of Ken and Margie Blanchard. He is an entrepreneur extraordinaire, *New York Times* and *BusinessWeek* bestselling author, and noted speaker. He began his career as a newspaper reporter covering stories in the Canadian Arctic, Japan, the United States, and Europe for such diverse media as the *Toronto Globe and Mail,* the Canadian Broadcasting Corporation, *Time,* the *Times* (London), and the *Winnipeg Free Press.* He left reporting to gain business experience and join Royal Canadian Securities, Ltd., where he rose to become a director and vice president. For fifteen years, Sheldon was CEO of Domo Gasoline Corporation, Ltd., which he built—along with Senator Douglas Everett, chairman—into one of Canada's largest independent gasoline retailers, with many hundreds of employees. At a time when the industry was going almost exclusively self-serve, they built their business and reputation on full-serve "Jump to the Pump"® service. It was his experience creating legendary service at Domo Gas that brought Sheldon to write, with Ken Blanchard, the bestselling book *Raving Fans.*

After leaving Domo, Sheldon—with three partners—turned a small manufacturing plant, Precision Metalcraft, Inc., into a multimillion-dollar business. This success experience led him to coauthor with Ken his second bestseller, *Gung Ho!* Sheldon and Ken realized that you can't create raving fan customers without having motivated, committed, gung-ho people.

Sheldon's writing success led him to develop a third career as a stimulating speaker with great take-home value. His desire to help other entrepreneurs led Sheldon to coauthor two other books with Ken, *Big Bucks!* and *High Five!* There is nothing Sheldon enjoys more than mentoring other young business leaders, especially his son Kingsley, daughter Patti, and his honorary adopted son, Aaron. Patti and her husband, Kristjan, have created a large commercial recycling company, Phoenix Recycling, and a successful Canadian document-storage and high-security document-destruction business, while Kingsley manages the family holding company and Aaron rebuilds jet engines.

We thank you, Charlie and Sheldon, for your unending positive influence, which has made our world a better place. May all the good you've done for others come back to you both a thousand times over. We know your influence through *The One Minute Entrepreneur* will make a real difference.

—Ken Blanchard and Don Hutson

Contents

Foreword

There's something about essentials that we all seem to ignore. When it comes to entrepreneurship, we get consumed by our vision and forget about the money. We get consumed with our customer and forget about our employees. We get consumed about life and forget about death. Isn't it strange how you and I can become so disconnected from the essentials? That's why I love this little book. It's a wonderful story about the essentials of entrepreneurship.

After years of studying entrepreneurship, I'm sure about one thing: Becoming a success story is easier said than done. Within any given year, close to 1 million people start a small business in the United States. Sadly, at least 40 percent of those businesses fail within the first year. Eighty percent of them will be out of business within five years, and 96 percent will have closed their doors before their tenth birthday.

One of the primary reasons small businesses fail is that they are started by technicians—people who are skilled at something and who enjoy doing that thing. Whether they are electricians, writers, photographers, or computer programmers, these people make the fatal mistake of continuing to do the work they're skilled at while ignoring other vital parts of the business.

The One Minute Entrepreneur will help you avoid that fatal mistake. In a parable as delightful as it is instructive, Blanchard and Hutson focus on three essentials you must attend to if you want to be a successful entrepreneur.

The first key is your finances. Many entrepreneurs go out of business because they don't know how to manage their money. Expenses exceed their sales, they don't collect their bills, and they don't realize that their success depends on cash, cash, cash.

The second key to entrepreneurial success involves your people. Empowering others to take responsibility in your business relieves you, the entrepreneur, of having to do everything yourself. Once your people feel empowered, they become like owners and are eager to take special care of customers.

Which brings us to Blanchard and Hutson's third vital element of entrepreneurial success: taking care of your customers. You can be the most skilled technician in the world, but if you don't take care of your customers, you're never going to make it.

The One Minute Entrepreneur will help you understand that while success might be easier said than done, focusing on a few essentials will dramatically increase your probability of success—and help you have fun doing it.

—Michael Gerber, entrepreneur and author of
The E-Myth, The E-Myth Revisited, and
Awakening the Entrepreneur Within

A Note to Readers

While *The One Minute Entrepreneur* is a fictional parable, a number of the advice givers in the story are real people. Why did we name them? Because we owe our success to mentors who seemed to come into our lives at the right time with the right advice—and we were smart enough to listen.

Why the *One Minute* Entrepreneur? Because we found the best advice we ever received was given in less than a minute. In other words, the gems in life did not come from long diatribes, but rather short, meaningful insights. Perhaps that's why *The One Minute Manager*—which is based on three simple secrets—has been on bestseller lists for more than twenty-five years.

The contribution that Ethan Willis brought to the book is the development of a comprehensive online assessment of twenty key attributes of successful entrepreneurs. These winning characteristics are listed in the appendix. To assess yourself on these key attributes, go to www.estrengths.com. This free assessment will help you get the most out of this book by helping you discover your entrepreneurial strengths.

Building a Firm Foundation

From the time he was a kid, Jud McCarley dreamed of owning his own business. Yet he nearly blew his opportunity before he even graduated from high school.

Jud was a good kid but an unremarkable student. In everything that counted most to him he was having a great senior year. He was popular, played tight end on a winning football team, and had a pretty girlfriend who thought the world revolved around him. That great year, however, was about to be interrupted.

On what started as a typical Saturday night, Jud took his girlfriend home from their date and drove to the Gridiron Grill to meet the boys. Tiring of the small talk, some of them decided to drive out to the gravel pit, where they could drink a couple of beers.

Jerry "Race" Nelson invited Jud to ride with him. Race wasn't a close friend, but Jud loved cars, and Jerry's new high-performance Mustang was incentive enough.

Jerry was charging down Holmes Road doing seventy-five in a forty-five-mile-per-hour zone, living up to his nickname, when he saw blue lights flashing. He pulled over, got out his license and registration, and looked sheepish as the officer approached the car.

"Get out of the car, son," the officer said.

Jerry obeyed. Jud sat still, wondering if he was supposed to get out or not. After giving Jerry a lecture and a speeding ticket, the officer leaned into the car to look at Jud.

"What about you? You always go along with what your buddies do?" the officer asked.

"Uh, I, uh," Jud began, but before he could form a complete sentence, the officer turned his attention to a small vinyl bag sticking out from under the driver's seat.

"What's that?" the officer asked.

"I don't know," Jud said.

"Maybe I'd better have a look," said the officer. He opened the door and took out the vinyl bag. "Sure looks like marijuana to me." He looked at Race and then back to Jud. "I think we'd better go down to the station and call your parents."

Wait! Had the officer just said "marijuana"? Jud's ears pounded with the beating of his heart. How could this be happening? He'd never done drugs! What would his parents say? What would everybody think if he had to go to jail? How was he going to talk his way out of this?

On the long, quiet drive to the police station, Jud and Jerry were both imagining all kinds of outcomes. Once there, the process was cut-and-dried. Jud realized that nobody was going to talk their way out of anything that night. They made their one phone call, were put in a cell, and began discussing how they could get out of there.

through a network of gay clerics. Sociologist James Wolf, a married layman, who edited the book, estimated that 20 percent of the priests in the United States are homosexual, half of them sexually active. In 1987, the Reverend John Yockey of Washington Theological Union said in the *National Catholic Reporter* that the number of gay priests was "from disproportionate to overwhelming. Forty percent would not be an unreasonable estimate."

332 two-thirds of Catholics: According to a poll by the *Sunday Press* of Dublin, the results of which were published in the *New York Daily News*, May 24, 1992.

332 "exorcist" syndrome: *Gay, Straight and In-between. The Sexology of Erotic Orientation*, by John Money, Oxford University Press, 1988, pp. 108–10.

332 ". . . standard-bearer of traditional sexual values": Ibid., p. 109.

332 Dr. Judith Becker: From interview with author, March 2, 1992.

333 "I don't think he'll ever admit . . .": From author's interview with Dr. Kennedy, April 1992.

EPILOGUE

338 The appearance of Covenant House after the scandal: From *The New York Times*, February 20, 1991, and from author's interviews with staff workers.

340 "No one has matched it": Author's interview with Robert McGrath, April 1992.

341 ". . . don't have a revolving door": *The New York Times*, February, 20, 1991.

341 "Covenant House is still in transition": *The New York Times*, February 20, 1991.

342 shelters are still too large and dangerous: Ibid.

The kid in the next cell overheard them and said, "This ain't TV jail, boys. When you come here you spend the night, no matter who you are or what you did or didn't do!" He sounded like a veteran of this environment. Jud sank further into his bunk.

Jud's father showed up early the next morning. After a stern lecture from his dad, Jud was feeling like a criminal.

"Dad," Jud said, "you raised me right, and you deserve better than being down here with me right now. I swear I didn't do drugs. I didn't even know Jerry smoked marijuana. I'm really sorry this happened."

Reginald McCarley, a sternly principled man, had a strong sense of right and wrong.

"Jud, I believe you. But I'm going to tell you something that I never want you to forget. Are you listening?"

"Yes, sir," Jud said.

His father looked him in the eyes. "When I was about your age, my uncle taught me that at any given time, we are becoming the average of the five people with whom we are most closely associated. Don't ever underestimate the importance of whom you choose to be with. And remember, when you have an opportunity to learn from someone who is exceptionally smart or successful, capture the gems they send your way."

It was a pivotal moment for Jud. Although he didn't realize it at the time, it would be the first of many meaningful insights he would learn over his lifetime. The incident taught him how lucky he was to have a loving, caring parent. It also led him to understand that if he associated with values-driven yet successful people, he couldn't help but improve himself.

* * *

After football practice Monday afternoon, Coach Knapp asked Jud to come into his office. Jud had an idea what the visit would be about, and he approached Coach Knapp's office with trepidation.

"Close the door and have a seat," the coach said.

Without a word, Jud lowered himself into a chair.

"I hear you had a rough weekend," the coach said, "and I want to say a few things I hope you'll remember. One of the hardest decisions I ever had to make was whether to take this coaching job or stay with a company I'd been with for eight years. I gave up what could have been a good career there, but I felt I could make more of a difference as a coach.

"Jud, you're popular, you're a decent student, and you're a pretty good football player. But every teacher you have is convinced you could do better. When are you going to make something of yourself, instead of jerking around drinking beer at that gravel pit?"

Jud felt like he'd been kicked in the stomach. He swallowed hard.

Coach Knapp continued, "You want to enjoy a successful life, right?"

"Yes, sir," Jud said.

"Then make this a turning point. You're a nice kid from a fine family. With all the remodeling my wife and I have done on our house, we've enjoyed doing business with your dad's lumber-supply company. You found out this weekend that you're not bulletproof, son. Now, I want to show you something."

The coach opened a drawer and pulled out a worn, blue linen book.

"My mother gave me this when I went away to college. She told me to take a minute every now and then to write down the important things that happened, and to put a star by the major lessons I learned, so that I could share them with her when I went home. I resisted at first, but before long I got into it, not only to keep the promise to my mother but to keep quotes I liked, things I learned, and thoughts about important decisions I made. To remember them better, I distill them down to their essence so that they take no longer than about one minute to read. It's a habit that has changed my life."

The coach pulled out a clean, new notebook and handed it to Jud.

"Try it. If you decide to make something of yourself, this can chronicle the best ideas you hear along life's way."

Jud respected the coach and was moved that he'd taken the time to have this talk with him. He left Knapp's stadium office that day committed to turning his life around and getting it back on a successful path.

Before he turned off his lights that night, he pulled out his new notebook and took a minute to write down the advice he'd gotten that week from his dad and his coach. Thinking about what his coach had told him about keeping them short and to the point, he decided to call them One Minute Insights.

The following weekend, Jud joined the family for Sunday dinner with his grandparents. The family hadn't told his grandfather about Jud's "incident," but they had given his grandmother a heads-up. Since she'd been a schoolteacher and a personnel director, nothing surprised her and few things got by her. While the others were visiting in the living room, Jud's grandmother took him into the kitchen for a chat.

"You're going off to college soon, Jud," she said, "and you'll be exposed to many people and ideas. You'll encounter crossroads—points where you'll need to make choices. Try your best to make good, well-thought-out decisions. Often the decisions you make when you are young are more important than those made later in life, because they have more years in front of them."

"I'll do my best," said Jud.

"Also, be guided by values such as integrity, love, honesty, and purposeful work, because they'll be the foundation your life is built on. Write your values down and make sure you read them every day. Then, when your gut tells you you've violated one, stop. Take note and get back on the right path." She paused, letting the advice sink in.

She continued, "Jud, your values are some of the most important things you will ever have. Don't ever squander an opportunity to do the right thing. You never need to cheat to win. Remember that what's right is more important than who is right. If you want a life of success and balance, your values will be the vehicles to get you there."

Her special caring and perspective as a grandmother made her an appealing mentor—even more so than a parent—to Jud. That night he headed straight for his notebook and added the gems his grandmother had sent his way to the One Minute Insights he'd gotten from his dad and coach.

One Minute Insights

☞ Associate with people you admire and can learn from.

☞ Keep a notebook of the wisdom you read, hear, and learn, and distill that learning into One Minute Insights.

☞ A good life is built on strong, solid values such as integrity, love, honesty, and purposeful work.

☞ You never need to cheat to win.

☞ What is right is more important than who is right.

Growing in Knowledge

Over the next few years, Jud studied hard and was near the top of his senior class at the University of Memphis, while holding down a part-time sales position at a clothing store. Lots of his friends had already accepted positions with major companies, but Jud wasn't 100 percent sure what to do next. He liked sales, but he dreamed of owning his own company. He took pride in the fact that as an independent contractor selling at the clothing store, he made two or three times the money others did in their part-time jobs.

Dr. Avery Tonning, Jud's sales and marketing professor, had arranged for Jud and some of the other business majors to periodically attend dinner meetings of the Sales & Marketing Executives of Memphis, where they had the opportunity to hear from speakers working in the sales profession.

When Dr. Tonning encouraged Jud to write down key ideas from the speeches, Jud smiled. He already had three books full of key thoughts, and he eagerly added speakers' ideas at every opportunity.

Dr. Tonning had appeared in Jud's life at the perfect time. Not only was he Jud's professor, he was his academic advisor as well. Knowing Jud's passion for sales, Dr. Tonning encouraged him to attend a seminar that Dirk Gardner, president of National Sales Forum, was staging locally.

When Jud arrived at the seminar, his expectations were pretty low. Most of the sales speakers he had heard in school were marginal presenters. But the moment Gardner burst onstage, Jud knew this was something altogether different. Within minutes, the audience was mesmerized. Jud had never seen or heard anything like this man before. As Gardner hammered home points about self-motivation, success in selling, and the virtues of the free-enterprise system, Jud felt chills go up his spine. He was more fired up than he had ever been in his entire life.

The seminar featured four noted speakers: Dr. Kenneth McFarland, Bill Gove, Charlie "Tremendous" Jones, and Zig Ziglar. Jud had never heard of them, but he figured if Gardner was the front man and these guys were supposed to be even better, this could be quite a day.

The first featured speaker, Tremendous Jones, exuded a genuine enthusiasm. His favorite word was—you guessed it—"tremendous." He used it so frequently that when people started calling him "Tremendous" years ago, it caught on.

Jones told his rapt audience, "Five years from now, you will be the same as you are today except for the people you meet and the books you read." He thundered, "If you're serious about success, you should develop a library of self-help books and works of literary giants! Once you decide you admire the content, the values, and the style of a writer, devour every one of that author's works."

Jud loved to read, so this would be no problem for him. He made a note to see what he could find in the university library.

Next up: Zig Ziglar. *Where do these guys get their names?* Jud wondered. With a dynamic delivery and homespun southern humor, Ziglar taught Jud, "You can get everything you want in life if you help enough other people get what they want." This struck a chord with Jud. He believed there were vast opportunities in selling when you were selling something you believed in.

At the dinner break, Jud went to the lobby and patiently waited in line to buy one of Tremendous Jones's books. The great man autographed it, and they spent a few minutes talking. Jud felt totally connected with his sincerity and warmth. He took Jones's card and asked if he could contact him later. To Jud's surprise, Jones said yes.

The third speaker was Bill Gove, the first president of the National Speakers Association. He was a sales expert, but with his ability to make the crowd laugh, he could have been a comedian. Talking about his humble beginnings, he said, "We were a big family in a small house. I never got to sleep alone until I got married!" The audience howled.

Gove offered his wisdom: "Everyone loves to buy, but they hate to be sold. Lead with your ears! Ask questions, assess needs, develop relationships. If you're really good at it, people will practically beat your door down to buy from you."

What a refreshing departure from the hard closes and high-pressure tactics Jud had heard about. Gove argued that selling was a great and honorable profession for those who did it right. In reality, everyone sells their ideas every time they open their mouth. So why not get good at it?

The wrap-up speaker was Dr. Kenneth McFarland, known as "the dean of American speakers." McFarland inspired Jud with his hopeful vision of the American free-enterprise system. At one point, McFarland looked over the podium, seemingly right at Jud. He motioned with his index finger and softly said, "Come here and let me tell you something." Jud was almost out of his seat when he realized that the entire audience was leaning forward.

McFarland said, "If you can sell and sell well, nobody can ever quarterback you out of a great future. Success can only occur when opportunity and preparation meet. Remember that, and you'll enjoy a life of high achievement."

Jud ignored the ache of writer's cramp as he took copious notes. His curiosity had turned into a passionate desire to fully develop his own gifts. While Jud dreamed of having his own successful business, as his dad did, he realized he needed to develop the necessary skills and experience. He also realized that his real area of passion was motivating others and helping them make their lives successful. He was a sponge for the advice these speakers were dispensing.

McFarland ended to a thunderous standing ovation. With his new insight about his real passion, Jud went in direct pursuit of the seminar's producer, Dirk Gardner.

His heart pumped hard as he approached the man. Why beat around the bush?

"Mr. Gardner," he said, "I'm Jud McCarley from Dr. Tonning's sales class. I graduate with a sales major from the University of Memphis in six weeks, and I want to go to work for you. This seminar was one of the greatest experiences I've ever had, and I think I can help you sell others on attending your events."

Gardner said, "Well, Jud, I'm delighted you're impressed with what we do. Let's you and I have breakfast in the morning."

* * *

Jud arrived ten minutes early for the breakfast appointment and requested a quiet table. Within moments, Dirk Gardner approached, flashing a wide smile.

"You're early," he said as he took his seat. "You're off to a good start."

Over coffee and omelets, Jud answered Gardner's questions about his background, skills, and beliefs. The more they talked, the more deeply Gardner probed.

"How do you deal with rejection and failure, Jud?" he asked.

"I'm focused on success, of course, but I guess I deal with rejection okay," said Jud.

"We all grow strongest in the crucible of adversity," said Gardner. "The single biggest salesmanship lesson you must learn is that periodic rejection is very much a part of the success process."

"How so?" Jud asked.

"No matter how good you are, you'll experience a lot of failure. The greatest sales professionals are those who experience a 'no' and immediately go on to their next call with total confidence, giving as good a presentation as they ever have, unfazed by the previous rejection. Sales champions know that success is not determined by how much verbiage you can dish out. It's all about how much rejection you are willing and able to eat! You must go through the nos to earn the right to experience the yeses."

"I've never thought about rejection like that, but I'm eager to put your advice into practice," said Jud.

Gardner asked, "Are you willing to travel into cities you've never been to, where you don't know a soul, and start selling with enthusiasm?"

"Yes, I am," Jud replied.

For the first time, Jud felt a tinge of nervousness. He thought of his boss at the clothing store, who had preached, "It's not what you know, but who you know that counts."

Jud asked Gardner what he thought of that concept.

"That cliché has been around for a long time," Gardner replied. "Who you know can be important, but what matters is who knows *you* and what they think of you—your confidence, your professionalism, and your belief in what you are selling."

Jud scribbled more notes. He realized that learning was cumulative. Things he'd learned in the past were being superseded by better information from a more knowledgeable source. He smiled as he finished his notes. Dirk Gardner was definitely handing him gems. Gardner motioned for the waiter to bring more coffee.

"I'm glad you're excited about our seminar business and that you benefited from the event yesterday," he said, "but you also need to be grounded in reality. You can't imagine how challenging it is to put all those people in those seats.

"When you're presenting the program to people," Gardner continued, "they're evaluating our offering by the job you do that day, not by the job our speakers will do later. They can only imagine what that day will be like; they don't have a clue of the actual power of the upcoming event. Your responsibility is not to sell it short. The only way they can benefit from our seminar is to be there, and that sales task is up to you. You must arouse curiosity in them along with a desire to be in attendance. Still interested?"

"Yes, sir," Jud said.

"Are you motivatable?"

"You bet!" Jud answered.

"Trainable?"

"Absolutely!"

"Jud, does this sound like the type of career you want to pursue?"

Jud smiled. "If that's an offer, the answer is yes!"

"If you'll do what I tell you to do, I'm convinced that you will succeed. I'm willing to mentor you on the sales process if you promise me you'll work hard and follow my direction."

On a deep level, Jud knew this was going to be more than a job; it was his future unfolding. He would be an independent contractor on commission. He knew that drill. He would seize the opportunity!

One Minute Insights

☞ You'll be the same year after year except for the people you meet and the books you read.

☞ You can get what you want in life if you help other people get what they want.

☞ Lead with your ears.

☞ Success occurs when opportunity and preparation meet.

☞ It's not who you know that counts; it's who knows *you* and what they think of you.

☞ When you feel moments impacting your destiny, seize the opportunity.

Learning the Craft

Jud's new job in promoting the workshops consisted of a two-stage selling process. First, he called on a sales organization, talked to the manager, and attempted to set up a half-hour presentation at the manager's upcoming sales meeting. Jud would give a sample talk—a prelude to the high-powered seminar they were bringing to town—and give his listeners an opportunity to make a reservation. He made a commission on the number of seminar enrollments he sold.

Dirk Gardner was no fool. He hired his new sales-people on a straight commission basis, so he had very little downside. He was confident enough in his selection process that he felt he could pick winners, and since his salespeople had to get good or go hungry, he was ensured of having a highly motivated team. He was committed to giving them everything they needed to succeed.

In his first two weeks, Jud made loads of calls, but for some reason, they weren't translating into many sales. Despite his enthusiasm, this new career wasn't taking off as he'd expected. He was learning a new type of humility.

No good mentor lets a new subject fail, so Dirk Gardner began an intense one-on-one coaching process with Jud.

"Jud," he said, "the humility you mentioned is not a bad thing, but a good thing. It is with humility that we admit we don't have all the answers. It's humility that gives us the desire for a higher degree of focus, and it's with that intense focus that we learn and grow."

"How, exactly, do I focus?" asked Jud.

"Remember that for every yes you get, you will probably have to endure eight to ten nos. Know your numbers and conversion rates. If you take care of your numbers, your numbers will take care of you. As one of my favorite business gurus, Dr. Peter Drucker, said, 'If you can measure it, you can manage it.'"

"Thanks," said Jud. "That gives me something solid to go on—know my numbers."

It would be one of the finest lessons Jud would learn. He kept up with his numbers with a vengeance. At any given time, he knew exactly what his conversion rate of prospects to buyers was. He remembered fondly his father's advice about seizing opportunities to learn from people you admire. Dirk Gardner was just such a person. With Gardner's input, Jud worked diligently to improve the content and delivery of his sales presentation. He was convinced that those two items, along with call count, would determine his success and help him to eventually start his own business.

* * *

But after four months of steady work, Jud hadn't made much money. He'd originally thought that to be successful in selling you just had to be cheerful, nice, and helpful. He was now learning how it worked in the big leagues. He continued to plug away with enthusiasm and focus and began to show some progress. But by year-end he still wasn't making as much money as most of his college buddies. It was hard work, and there seemed to always be some financial pressure. He found that making the transition from naive student to productive sales professional wasn't all that easy.

With the next big seminar a month away in Philadelphia, Jud pulled out the business card from Tremendous Jones and dialed his number. He wondered if the popular speaker would even remember him, let alone make time for a meal together before the seminar.

"Of course I remember you, young man!" Tremendous boomed over the phone. "I'm pleased you followed up. That's half the battle—suiting up and showing up."

The night before the seminar, they were shaking hands at a restaurant. Knowing how busy Tremendous was, Jud deeply appreciated every moment he could share with him. So the second they sat down, Jud started to talk business.

"Hey, slow down!" said Tremendous. "We'll have time to talk business later. Tell me about you."

Jud filled in Tremendous on his life, hopes, and dreams about his passion for motivating others, and his long-term goal of creating his own motivational business.

Tremendous replied, "Jud, you're in the enviable position of simultaneously getting sales experience and speaking experience. You will learn a lot in this business. The sky is the limit as to where you can go."

Jones's words stirred hope in Jud. As a newcomer to the business world he'd believed the sky was the limit, but in the last few months that dream had been fading. A streak of recent rejections had shaken his confidence. Faith, hope, and optimism were being crowded out by fear, pessimism, and self-doubt.

Tremendous said, "I can see concern and doubt in your face. Don't get discouraged. Being a successful businessperson is a journey. And you've only just begun. Remember that whatever kind of business you intend to create—whether in sales or service, whether you're creating a dry-cleaning business, health-food store, or data-technology company—your fears will subside as you master the basics of business."

Realizing that Tremendous was right, Jud mustered the courage to ask the bold question he had been thinking about for weeks. "Charlie, would you consent to being a mentor to me? Dirk is my mentor on selling skills, but I'd love to have your input on a broader business perspective. I really want to grow, and you're already one of my role models."

Tremendous smiled broadly. "You've passed the first test. Mentors tend not to show up unless you ask them to. And since I'm already in the loop, I guess we should formalize the arrangement!"

"Thanks," said Jud. "I appreciate your generosity."

"It's called 'giving back,'" said Tremendous. "I wouldn't be where I am today without my mentors. I'll be one of your mentors, Jud, but there's something you should know: I take life in small bites. We won't spend a lot of time together, but I can pack a lot of information into just a minute."

"Funny you should say that," Jud responded with a smile. "My old coach taught me to take a minute every now and then to write down what's important. I have several notebooks full now. I call them my One Minute Insights, because most of the important things I've learned are short sound bites, not long diatribes."

"That's tremendous!" he boomed. "Then we're off to a good start. Now you have to promise me that I'm not tackling this project alone. I learned a long time ago that to be an effective mentor, you must first have an enthusiastic protégé. You already know where I stand on the importance of reading. It's the books you read and the people you meet that impact you the most. I want your commitment that you'll become a voracious reader. That doesn't necessarily mean you'll read a great number of books, but it does mean you'll read deeply for understanding. I have several literary mentors, and you should, too. You've got to agree to read every week. Is that a deal?"

"You bet," Jud said. He loved books, so this was an easy deal to make.

"I also want you to agree to spend time sharing with others the things I share with you. Helping others is just as important as being helped," said Tremendous. "Are you in?"

"I'm in," said Jud.

"Good," said Tremendous. "You'll get more out of my mentoring by making and honoring commitments like these."

After talking for a few more minutes about Jud's challenges in selling seminar enrollments, Tremendous wrapped up their discussion with one last piece of wisdom.

"Psych yourself up before every meeting with client groups. Be your best every time. You're on stage, so act like it! When you put energy and conviction into your presentation, your overall message will constantly improve. Great salespeople give every effort their best shot!"

Jud thought about all the rejections he'd been dealing with lately. "How do you get psyched up?" he asked.

"Great question," replied Tremendous. "When I was selling full-time, I would imagine making the sale—seeing my clients wearing big smiles as we shook hands after signing the deal. Now that I'm mainly a speaker, I do a similar thing. I imagine the audience leaping to their feet for a standing ovation at the end of my speech and clapping enthusiastically.

"There's been a lot of research on Olympic athletes," Tremendous continued. "The ones who tend to win are the ones who—before the race—see themselves sailing across the finish line, winning the race."

"What a great concept," said Jud. He smiled, realizing that Tremendous was indeed going to be a tremendous mentor.

One Minute Insights

☞ Humility helps you to be open to learning and growing in your field of expertise.

☞ Take care of your numbers and your numbers will take care of you.

☞ To create a successful business, you must first master the basics.

☞ For a mentor to be effective, you have to be an enthusiastic and committed protégé.

☞ Always visualize your desired outcome ahead of time.

☞ In sales and in every other business, you are constantly on stage—so act like it.

Catching the Entrepreneurial Bug

After three years at the National Sales Forum, Jud was like a racehorse kicking at its stall door. He wanted to get out on the track and run. He'd learned a vital skill—how to sell. He was doing his job well and was making a decent living. Yet Jud was ambitious; he wanted more. He felt driven to start his own company. He liked his boss and appreciated what Dirk had done for him, but he could see that working for him indefinitely would only hold him back. Nevertheless, he was afraid he would fail. He knew that tens of thousands of entrepreneurs before him—including Dirk—had faced these same doubts and forged ahead. But Jud wasn't sure he was enough of a risk taker.

So he called Tremendous to ask for his advice.

"Your being self-employed is inevitable," said Tremendous. "This has been your dream for years. The big question is, what kind of business are you going to develop? Sheldon Bowles, a great entrepreneur and author, says that when you want to start a business, you have to play to your passion. This is what Sheldon called the test of joy. What do you like to do most? If you try to be an entrepreneur just to make money and not to satisfy the fire in your belly, you will fail. If you don't love what you're doing, you will never put in the necessary time to be the best.

"Jud," continued Tremendous, "what have you been doing for National Sales Forum that you really love?"

"What I love to do is motivate others," Jud replied. "And I do that through speaking. Technically, I'm a sales-person. But I think my speaking ability has been my best sales asset, because that's what I love to do the most. When I get face-to-face with a customer to present our program, I can usually close a sale. People say I'm a good communicator. I've had the opportunity to give some speeches outside my work. I do a talk called 'So You Want to Sell Something?' It's an overview of all the things I've learned about selling from Dirk and my work at the National Sales Forum. But what I really love about it is that it's not just about sales. It's about positive motiva-tion—including self-motivation—and people get excited by it."

"How do you feel when you're on your feet in front of a group?"

"Energized! I have to be careful, because I lose track of time, I love it so much. That's why my dream has been to start my own speaking business, crazy as that might sound."

"I don't think you're crazy, Jud. Every business starts with a dream. The bigger the dream, the bigger the potential. That's why I became a speaker. I want to help others, and I'd rather sell myself than someone else or some product."

That's all Jud needed to hear. "Judson McCarley and Associates," he said proudly.

Tremendous laughed. "Now let me give you another piece of advice. Don't resign your sales job with Dirk until you have some outside speaking success under your belt. This gets to a second thing I learned from Sheldon. You need to find people who will pay for your passion. Sheldon called it the test of purpose. At some point, making money has to be more important than having fun. That's when you have to ask this question: Will anybody give you money to do what you love? It might take you a little time to develop a couple of inspiring speeches that people will want to pay to listen to and learn from. If nobody will pay you to speak, you have a hobby, not a business. I sing at the top of my lungs in the shower, but Gloria and I would be on Skid Row if I tried to make a living as a singer."

"What do you suggest I do next?" asked Jud.

"First, join Toastmasters. I'm sure there's a chapter where you live. They meet over breakfast and give everybody a chance to make short speeches and get feedback. They're a wonderful group, and you'll learn a lot.

"Second, see if you can get some time off the second week of next month, because I'll take you as my guest to the National Speakers Association convention. They love people who want to get into their business. You'll be able to network with some wonderful speakers from around the country."

"Done!" said Jud.

One Minute Insights

☞ Ambition is the fuel that can drive life-changing events.

☞ Identify what you're passionate about doing. Look to do more of it.

☞ Don't be afraid to dream big.

☞ Don't quit your day job until you've got some success under your belt.

☞ If nobody will pay you to do what you love, you have a hobby, not a career.

Gaining a Vital Teammate

The following month, Jud caught a flight to Orlando to join Tremendous Jones at the annual meeting of the National Speakers Association. When he arrived at the convention hall, the room buzzed with energy. Jud felt his pulse quicken as he recognized some of the famous authors and speakers he'd admired for years: Denis Waitley, Brian Tracy, Stephen Covey, Harvey Mackay, and Patrick Lencioni.

He scanned the meeting rooms and finally spotted Tremendous chatting with an attractive young woman in a smart-looking suit.

"Jud," said Tremendous with a big grin, "I'd like you to meet Terri Aviotti, the director of training for Crandall Industries and a fine speaker in her own right."

"Hi," Terri said, extending a hand. "Good to meet you, Jud." Terri's sharp blue eyes seemed to look right through Jud, and her smile melted his heart.

"The pleasure is mine," said Jud, shaking her hand. He felt an immediate attraction to Terri and had to remind himself that his focus was embarking on his new speaking business. He was certainly not in the market for a relationship. His business was the love of his life. A romantic involvement would just get in his way. All his attention was directed toward building his skills and his business, and that's the way he intended to keep it.

Yet, of all the important contacts he made at the convention, the one who really captured Jud's attention was Terri. It wasn't just her eyes; she had a wonderful presence as well. And he loved talking to her. As he spent more time with her during the convention, he realized that she was one of the smartest and most dynamic people he'd ever met, as attractive on the inside as she was on the outside. On the last day of the convention, they exchanged business cards.

Two weeks later they met in Atlanta, where Crandall Industries was headquartered. Terri's company was always looking for good motivational speakers, and she wanted to talk to Jud about what he and National Sales Forum might have to offer. During their business lunch, Jud discovered that he and Terri admired many of the same role models and shared many of the same values. In fact, they laughed when they both realized that it was their grandmothers who had emphasized the importance of honesty and integrity. Their working lunch and afternoon meeting advanced through dinner. As Jud left Terri at the end of the day, he was racking his brain to think of how he could see her again. He kept trying to put her out of his mind, but he could never do it for long, and he found himself thinking about the next time they'd meet.

The two began to see each other as regularly as their busy schedules would allow. It eventually became difficult to justify commuting to Atlanta every week to support their relationship. Each time he and Terri talked on the phone, Jud hated to hang up.

One day, Tremendous called and put Jud on the spot.

"When are you going to get serious about that wonderful woman I introduced to you?" he asked.

"I adore Terri," Jud said, "but marriage is a pretty big step. How do I know I'm making the right choice?"

"I'll give you a piece of advice I learned at age fifteen from my uncle," said Tremendous. "We were out on the lake, fishing for bass. My uncle told me that it's okay to fall in love with looks and personality, but to marry character. He told me to go for a 'long-term horse,' not a short-termer. Does that help clarify things?"

"Yes," said Jud, "it does. Terri's got it all—especially the character. Honesty and integrity are key values in her life. She values family as well as work that makes a difference in people's lives. Patience and loyalty are also way up on her list. I think she's a long-termer."

In the end, love overcame any fears Jud might have had about a relationship interfering with his dreams. During the following Christmas holidays, Jud and Terri spent time in the home of Tremendous and Gloria Jones, gathered around the piano singing Christmas carols with close friends. On the way home, filled with love and Christmas spirit, Jud proposed to Terri. Six months later, they were married and living in their own place in Jud's hometown, Memphis.

* * *

Jud had always imagined that when he broke through the glass ceiling into his life as a successful entrepreneur, he'd do it alone. Terri, too, had planned to continue developing her career as a director of training. But that all changed when, shortly after they said "I do," good friends suggested they go to a workshop for couples called Marriage Encounter®. This was an intensive weekend where spouses learned a wonderful way to communicate.

They were asked to write letters on various topics, starting with "What I really like about you is . . ." and ending the weekend with an epistle on "Why I choose to spend the rest of my life with you." After each had finished writing a letter, they were asked to exchange them with a hug. So Terri read Jud's letter, and he read hers. When they had finished reading each other's thoughts, they had to decide who went first. For example, with the letter about what they liked about each other, if Terri went first, she would tell Jud all the things he said he liked about her until he agreed that's what he'd said. Then it was his job to tell Terri what she really liked about him until she agreed. They were impressed by how much this helped them listen to each other.

While the strategy Jud and Terri learned was helpful, what impacted them the most was a discussion about "married singles." These were people who ate meals together and slept together but led two separate lives, and never the twain did meet. The Marriage Encounter facilitators suggested that healthy couples spend at least 30 percent of their waking hours doing things together. They argued, "Why be on different PTA committees? Why have one coach Little League sports without the other? When you do things together, you get to bask in each other's strengths and your relationship becomes richer."

That advice hit home with Jud and Terri. They decided that rather than developing separate careers, one day they would build a speaking business together. They would be a team.

One Minute Insights

☞ On the entrepreneurial path, few people come into your life without a reason.

☞ Becoming a successful entrepreneur and having a spouse are not mutually exclusive.

☞ When it comes to finding a life partner, character and values trump personality and looks.

☞ To build a great marriage, especially if you're an entrepreneur, make sure you commit to spending time together outside of meals and sleeping.

☞ You and your spouse are a team. Act like one.

A Door Opens

While building a world-famous speaking business together was Jud and Terri's new dream, the reality of their early business life fell far short of that vision. Financial considerations kept Jud with National Sales Forum, while Terri found another opportunity in the training department of a nearby firm. It became apparent that to start their own company, they needed a break.

A door opened one fall when Jud and Terri were invited to participate in a weeklong university in San Francisco for the Entrepreneurs' Organization, EO. An organizer for the event, Red O'Rourke, had heard Jud speak at a National Speakers Association meeting. He'd been so impressed with Jud's youthful charisma that he invited him to speak at the EO event in San Francisco. Jud was between seminars at the National Sales Forum, so he was able to take a weeklong vacation.

Jud had an inkling this might be the opportunity he'd been praying for. He was to be one of forty faculty members who would be speaking to approximately six hundred EOers and their spouses. The faculty resources included Wayne Dyer, Jim Collins, Jim Rohn, Tom Peters, and other luminaries. Jud could hardly believe it. He'd love to get their autographs, let alone be on the faculty with them.

When Jud told Red O'Rourke that his wife also was a speaker, Red asked to see some video footage of her on the platform. After seeing Terri in action, Red immediately asked her to do a special session on balance—her specialty—as part of their lifestyle track.

The first day of the university, Jud was ready. He poured all his years of preparation into his well-honed motivational speech "So You Want to Sell Something?" and about two hundred of the twelve hundred university attendees showed up. EOers and their spouses could choose either three or four sessions every class period. When Jud finished his session, he got the standing ovation he had visualized. The audience loved it and went racing out of the room buzzing with enthusiasm about the dynamic new speaker. Jud was stunned by the positive response.

"Why not?" said Terri as she hugged him. "It didn't just happen. Look at all the early breakfast meetings of Toastmasters you attended, and all the coaching you got there, plus the support your new National Speakers Association buddies have given you. Not to mention the hundreds of presentations you've given to small groups promoting the seminars."

"I guess you're right, hon. I did put a lot of hours into creating exciting speeches."

Terri said with a smile, "Tremendous would be proud of you."

On the second day, Terri did her session titled "Strategies for Balancing Complicated Lives" and also received rave notices from the entrepreneurs and spouses who attended.

Jud high-fived Terri and gave her a hug. "Way to go!"

The third day, Jud gave a talk on leadership. This time about eight hundred people showed up. On Friday—the final day of the university—Jud did another session on strategies for managing change, and essentially the whole convention came.

At the end of the university, Red O'Rourke said, "Well, Jud, you won. You were the most popular speaker, and Terri hit a home run, too. What are you two going to do now?"

Jud said, "Terri and I both have to get back to our jobs."

Red said, "You're crazy. When you're hot, you're hot! I've been talking to some of the EOers here. We think you two are ready to start your own speaking and training company."

Jud smiled. "That's certainly our dream. We want to have our own speaking business someday, but right now we don't see how it's financially possible. We have enough trouble balancing our checkbook. How are we going to run a company?"

"Don't throw away your dream," said Red. "I think you guys have the determination and guts to step out on your own."

* * *

When Jud told Terri about his conversation with Red, they both felt torn but excited. They wanted to have their own business, but they were afraid.

"Starting our own company now could be our moment of destiny—or it could be our moment of doom!" Jud said. "I'm just afraid that if we dive in and fail, we'll prove all the naysayers right."

Terri nodded. "We're definitely at a crossroads," she said.

Jud suddenly remembered the day in his grandmother's kitchen years ago when she told him how important it was to think through such decisions with care. He knew that they were being given a choice, and that the decision they made about this would affect their life for years to come. Starting his own business had been his dream for years. But could he and Terri pull it off? Did they have the experience? If ever he needed his mentor, it was now.

That evening, Jud called Tremendous.

"What's up, Jud?" Tremendous asked.

"Terri and I are here at an EO university in San Francisco. Apparently, our performances here were good enough that a group of influential businesspeople is encouraging us to start our own speaking and training business right now."

"So you both were hits?" Tremendous asked.

"I gave three speeches and the crowds increased every time. For my final talk, I essentially drew the whole convention. Terri gave her specialty speech on balance and wowed them. To hear these people talk, we're the best thing since sliced bread."

"So they think you're ready to start your own business?"

"Yes. Several presidents offered to get us plenty of speaking opportunities over the next year or so. What do we do, Tremendous?"

"I'm excited for you, Jud," said Tremendous. "If you are really ready to start your own business, you need to know what it takes to be a successful entrepreneur. I recommend that you call a friend of mine, Harris Palmer. He's an entrepreneur from Australia who's forgotten more than most people know about starting a business. He certainly helped me."

* * *

The next morning, Jud dialed the number Tremendous had given him for Harris Palmer. He was amazed when he got right through.

"If you're a friend of Tremendous, you can't be all bad. How can I help you?" said Harris in his thick Australian brogue.

"I want to start my own business, and Tremendous says you can do that in your sleep. Do you have any pointers for me?"

"This is going to be a short conversation," said Harris, "because there are only four things to remember to be a successful entrepreneur.

"First, your sales have to exceed expenses. A lot of people, when they start a business, want to get fancy stationery and business cards and a nice office, and they don't have any customers. That's a formula for disaster.

"Second, collect your bills. There are all kinds of people who go out of business with other people owing them money. Be reasonable, but don't be your customers' banker.

"Third, take care of your customers. They pay your bills and write your checks. Remember: You work for them.

"Fourth, take care of your people. I'm amazed at the number of entrepreneurs who abuse their people and then expect them to take care of their customers. As you build your business, your people are not your company's most important asset. They are your company. When you shut the doors at the end of the day and your people head home, your business goes with them."

Jud was frantically scribbling notes as Harris talked.

"Wow," he said. "Tremendous was right about you. What great advice on starting a business. Thanks!"

* * *

Shortly after the conversation with Harris, Jud and Terri moved ahead with their dream and began to formulate a plan for their new company, JTA—Judson, Terri & Associates. They decided to keep it simple—no fancy business cards or stationery, or even an office. After they had enough money coming in, all of that would take care of itself.

They were energized, but scared as well. They debated the pros and cons for hours on end. On the plus side, they were fulfilling a dream they passionately shared. On the negative side, they'd be putting at risk what little financial security they had. Giving up two paychecks was a risk-taking move.

Fortunately, their optimism overshadowed their fear. They called Tremendous on a speakerphone to share Jud's conversation with Harris and their excitement about launching their new business.

"Harris was great," said Jud. "We've been back and forth about this next move, but we've finally decided we're ready to take the plunge!"

"We're totally committed now and there's no turning back," added Terri enthusiastically. "What do you think, Tremendous?"

There was a pause on the other end of the line. Then Tremendous shouted, "Rev up your engines—it's time to take off!"

One Minute Insights

☞ Too many people dream too small. Remember, you'll never achieve more than you think you can. So create a big dream.

☞ When opportunity knocks, seize it.

☞ Never let your expenses outstrip your revenue.

☞ Don't be a banker for your customers. Timely collection of invoices is crucial.

☞ Your customers are a company's lifeblood—they pay the bills.

☞ Nurture your people. They make it all happen. Without them, you have no company.

Launching the Company

Jud dreaded turning in his resignation. As much as he'd longed to break free, Dirk had become like a father to him. Without Dirk's encouragement, Jud never would have found his passion.

Any fear he had about Dirk's reaction vanished when his old boss leaped to his feet, ran around the desk, and gave Jud a hug.

"Tremendous told me this was inevitable, especially when you picked up such a vital teammate as Terri," Dirk said.

Then Dirk did the unimaginable. He returned to his desk, reached into a bottom drawer, pulled out his checkbook, and wrote Jud a check for five thousand dollars. "Maybe you and Terri could put this to good use as you get started," he said with a smile. "I can't tell you how much I appreciate all you have done for me and the National Sales Forum."

Jud was speechless. He thought about a good friend of his, who'd been given twenty minutes to clear out his desk after he resigned. His eyes welled with tears as he said to Dirk, "I'm so blessed to have a mentor and friend as wonderful as you. How can I thank you?"

"The best thanks you can give me is to succeed and be two of the best speakers in the country," said Dirk, giving him a hug.

"We are certainly going to give it the old college try," said Jud with a smile. "Any parting advice?"

"Never ask a person who's hooked on mentorship for advice unless you want some," said Dirk with a twinkle in his eye. "Two thoughts: Watch your ego. If you get too many standing ovations and people hanging on your every word, you might start to believe your own press. We once hired a speaker who was great on the platform but had such an enormous ego he was impossible to work with. We were considering him for twelve seminar appearances, but canceled him after the first one. So be competent, but also be a person of humility."

"And your second piece of advice?" asked Jud.

"You may have given the same speech many times before. But deliver it each time with the same passion and enthusiasm as if it were your first," said Dirk. "What you're speaking about might be familiar to you, but it's probably not to your audience. If you touch just one person's life, that may be the reason you're there."

Jud couldn't believe it. Not only was Dirk not angry, but he was generous beyond imagination and still willing to mentor Jud with good advice.

* * *

That night, Jud and Terri both signed the JTA incorporation papers. As the ink dried, Jud reached over and held Terri's hand. "From the moment you walked into my life," he said, "you've helped make my dreams come true. This is what I've always wanted, Honey—my own company. I love the fact that we get to do it together."

She squeezed his hand and dazzled him with her smile. "Give credit where credit is due. If you hadn't dreamed it, we wouldn't have achieved it."

With that, JTA was born.

Jud called Red O'Rourke to tell him about their decision. Red said, "I'm thrilled for you both. If you ever need any help, I'm only a phone call away."

* * *

The first decision Jud and Terri had to make about JTA was who was going to play what role in running the company. They felt that Jud's strong suit was the visionary or strategic part of leadership. He was purposeful and able to dream big dreams. Terri's strengths, on the other hand, were in the operational aspect of the company. She was a resourceful organizer and manager of people. For those reasons, Jud became the chairman of JTA and Terri became president and chief operating officer.

In the beginning, Jud and Terri ran JTA out of their house. It was a real mom-and-pop operation. They kept the office supplies in their hall cupboards and stored and mailed handouts for their speeches from their garage. Kinko's was their only office.

As they had promised, their EO friends helped to keep Jud and Terri busy. They even booked them for the next EO university, which would be held in Melbourne, Australia, in the fall. Jud and Terri felt honored and blessed by their support.

While the EO support was helpful, it was not sufficient. Jud and Terri had to work hard to secure other speaking events. As word about how good they were spread, so did awareness of their business.

After about six months, JTA's cash flow was good enough to allow Jud and Terri to lease some office space. They had just enough room for two small work areas. They hired an office manager/secretary, which left a cramped space for Jud and Terri to share.

Jud and Terri thought often about the advice Jud had received from Harris Palmer. They did everything they could to ensure that sales always exceeded expenses. Linda, their office manager/secretary, worked diligently to collect their bills and make sure they were paid for the work they did.

While Jud and Terri occasionally were scheduled to speak on the same programs, such as EO events, they often headed off in different directions. Sometimes it seemed like they were ships passing in the night. A couple of decisions changed that.

First, Jud and Terri realized that if the only way they could make money was for them to speak in person, their income was limited by the number of speaking events they could squeeze in. Moreover, their bodies would eventually wear out. So they came up with a new vision: They wanted to make money while they slept. They imagined what it would be like if checks were working their way through the mail system while they were resting. So they decided to expand their business, and they called Tremendous for ideas.

"Slowly expanding your business is a great idea," said Tremendous. "When it comes to making money, there's a third thing Sheldon Bowles taught me. You have to plus your passion. He called that the test of creativity. How do you create new avenues of revenue that build on your passion? Always remember that your income is a function of revenue minus expenses. Unfortunately, when it comes to increasing their income, most people focus all their attention on cutting costs."

"Isn't it important to manage your costs?" Terri asked.

"Absolutely," said Tremendous. "But while managing costs is important, it can be a negative energy drain."

"That's for sure," said Jud.

"To counter that," Tremendous continued, "you need to put positive energy into creating those new avenues of revenue that build off what you already are passionate about and good at doing."

To build the business beyond themselves, Jud and Terri knew they would need help. Jud called Red O'Rourke to tell him what they were up to. Red agreed to organize an advisory board for JTA that could help them through this next stage of development.

He recruited three other EOers to join him on the new advisory board. Each of them had a different strength area to bring to the new business: Juan Escobar had a passion for financial matters; Lou Stafford, for customer service; and Nancy Kaline, for people development. Red would be the convener and go-to guy. They agreed to fly at their own expense to join Red, Jud, and Terri later that month at a resort near Jud and Terri's hometown of Memphis. The purpose of the meeting was to develop a business plan for expanding the company. Jud and Terri were asked to do some thinking about their goals and strategies before the meeting.

When Jud and Terri shared their initial thoughts about expanding their business at the meeting a month later, their EO friends kidded them, because they'd left out an important detail. The two young entrepreneurs talked about working with people they loved, making a difference in the world, and having fun. Nowhere was there any mention of making a profit.

"Who's going to pay for all this expansion?" asked Juan with a laugh. "Making a profit is a necessity if you want to continue to stay in business."

"Juan is right," said Red. "While profit should not be your only focus, without good cash management, you are in trouble."

That weekend, not only did their EO friends help them clarify their goals so they became real business goals, but they also helped them develop a budget, analyze staff needs, and create a comprehensive business plan.

* * *

Jud and Terri began to implement their new business plan right away. First they partnered with some other speakers they could book when Jud or Terri either couldn't make an event or weren't a perfect fit for it. For their efforts, they would get 25 percent of the fee. They essentially became a small speakers' bureau.

Second, Jud and Terri began to develop some learning materials—assessment instruments, audios, and videos—that would enhance their programs and that they could sell to clients and other speakers.

New strategies such as these required additional staff, which they slowly began to add, making sure that expenses didn't exceed revenues.

The new businesses and resources also needed supervision, which was hard when Jud and Terri were both gone from the office. But that all changed when Terri became pregnant with their first child.

Morning sickness initially limited Terri's travel schedule, and then the arrival of Alex put a real halt to her speaking career. Except for local speaking opportunities, both Jud and Terri decided that it didn't make sense to have Terri away from home. That decision made even more sense when five months later Terri became pregnant again, and nine months after that Alex's sister, Elizabeth, was born. Now Terri stayed home to manage the company while the heavy lifting for their business fell on Jud's shoulders.

One Minute Insights

☞ Unless you want to do all the work, you have to think of ways to come up with new sources of revenue.

☞ If you focus only on managing costs, your business will never grow.

☞ Don't be afraid to seek advice when your business goes to a new level.

☞ Making a profit is always a necessity if you want to stay in business.

Financial Growing Pains

Over the next five years, the company slowly grew to fifteen employees and ten affiliate speakers. During that period, Jud and Terri moved their offices twice. It wasn't always easy, and Jud's youthful dream of vast riches was still a long way off.

When the economy hit a downturn, the numbers did not look good at all. While all the work Jud and Terri had done to increase sales had worked, they began to lose sight of some of the basics they'd learned early on. Expenses had risen faster than income. Not only were expenses exceeding sales, but JTA's accounts receivable were way behind, too. Some of their biggest clients were delinquent on bills, and on average, invoices were being paid far beyond the standard thirty-day period.

Jud knew it was time to go see Juan Escobar, the member of their advisory board who knew the most about finances. When Jud sat down in Juan's office, he was quick to admit, "We seem to have forgotten the first two things that Harris Palmer told us were required to be a successful entrepreneur: Our sales have to exceed expenses, and we have to collect our bills."

Juan smiled. "I'm so glad you admit that, Jud. I tried to warn you earlier, but I'm only a member of your advisory board. You and Terri make the final decisions. You were so caught up in your growth efforts that you chose not to listen.

"If you remember, I told you at our first meeting, when you were just getting started, that making it in business requires three very important things."

The expression on Jud's face suggested that if Juan had told them, he had forgotten.

Juan said, "This time, I want you to write these down—in capital letters."

Jud reached for his legal pad. "I'm ready," he said.

"CASH, CASH, CASH. That's what it takes to make it in business! A healthy profit has to be a team effort. While increasing revenue is important, everyone has to watch the margins by managing costs and collecting receivables. Jud, it doesn't matter how smart you are or how innovative your products are if you don't get paid in a timely manner. You must collect your receivables right away. Without good cash management, you'll never make it. You've got to solve this problem immediately. Right now I think you've got about three months before your banks and other collection agents start calling."

"I agree, Juan," said Jud. "What do you suggest?"

"We need to design a short-term plan to stop the financial bleeding. And you need to open the books to everyone in the company."

At first, Jud resisted opening the financials to everyone.

"I know what you're thinking," said Juan. "If you're like most managers, the last thing you want to do is share financial information with your people. But smart managers realize that large financial gains can be made by sharing what used to be considered sensitive data. They believe that when people understand the business realities of how their company makes money, they are much more apt to roll up their sleeves and help out. When this happens, everyone feels a sense of ownership, because they begin to realize how their efforts impact the company's bottom line.

"I'll give you an example," continued Juan. "Back in the days when I owned a restaurant, I was having a hard time convincing my general manager about the merits of sharing important financial data with employees. To unfreeze my manager's thinking, I went into the restaurant one night at closing time and asked everyone to join me in the dining room. I divided all the employees—cooks, dishwashers, waiters, waitresses, bus people—into groups of five or six around tables and asked them to come to an agreement about the answer to this question:

"'Of every sales dollar that comes into this restaurant, how many cents do you think fall to the bottom line—money that can be returned to the investors as profit or reinvested into the business?'

"The least amount any group guessed was forty cents. Several groups guessed seventy cents. In a restaurant, the reality is that if you can keep five cents on the dollar, you are doing well. Ten cents, and you're ecstatic! Can you imagine the attitude among my employees toward such things as wasted food, labor costs, and breakage if they thought our restaurant was a money machine?" asked Juan.

"I bet that changed the way they behaved," said Jud.

"It did," Juan replied. "One of the cooks said, 'You mean, if I burn a steak that costs us six dollars and we sell it for twenty, at a 5 percent profit margin we have to sell six steaks for no profit to make up for my mistake?' He had things figured out."

"I see your point," said Jud. "But opening the books just doesn't feel comfortable, especially when the numbers aren't all that great."

"That's because you're more concerned about looking successful than getting help to be successful. If you keep your people well informed and let them use their brains, you'll be amazed how much they'll help manage costs and brainstorm ways to increase revenues," said Juan.

The following week, Jud and Terri carried out Juan's suggestion by calling an all-company meeting. They opened the books and shared the balance sheet. The numbers were pretty grim. Seeing the concern on people's faces, Jud said to everyone, "Terri and I, in turning around this situation, don't want to get rid of people. We want to solve this together. We intend to form several task forces to look into how we can continue to increase our sales, as well as suggest how we can cut our costs. It's clear to us that we need to reduce expenses by 25 to 30 percent over the next quarter to dig our way out of this."

Excited that Jud and Terri were so open and honest, everyone jumped in with both feet to help out. They agreed that everyone would take a salary cut. Jud and Terri took a 15 percent cut in pay, and all the key managers took 10 percent cuts. All the frontline employees followed suit, with a 5 percent cut. Everyone also agreed to a number of other cost-cutting measures. For example, if someone left the company, they wouldn't replace that person. And during this turnaround period, JTA would not match contributions to the employees' 401(k) funds.

Jud and Terri were amazed by the loyalty and commitment they received from their people during this hard time. Everyone was willing to tighten their belts for as long as it took to turn the company around. To everyone's surprise, the financial turnaround took less than eighteen months.

Jud told Tremendous Jones the good news. Predictably, he said, "Tremendous!" He added, "Now that you have the finances under control, don't forget the last two things that Harris Palmer told you about successful entrepreneurs: Take care of your customers, and take care of your people. In fact, I heard a wonderful saying recently that pulls all this together: Profit is the applause you get for taking care of your customers and creating a motivating environment for your people."

"That is a good one," said Jud.

"As I've said, you've already made some good moves with your finances. But how are you doing with your customers and your people?"

Jud swallowed hard. Business had come back with a vengeance, but he knew well that they didn't have the systems set up to handle all the customer demand they were now getting. He was afraid they could blow a good thing. While their people were excited about their contribution to turning the company around financially, they were getting burned out from working long hours. Plus, they were rushing to fulfill orders and making a lot of mistakes. There were far too many instances of shipping the wrong materials to the wrong people. Jud realized they were putting lots of folks on hold for too long.

"We need to do better," he replied.

That night, Jud told Terri about his conversation with Tremendous. "We have to develop some strategies for serving our customers better and getting our people the help and support they need to effectively implement those strategies," he told Terri.

Later that week, Terri realized firsthand the problems they were having when she overheard one of their staff members, Maria, taking care of a phone call in a manner so perfunctory it almost sounded cold.

"Crank caller?" Terri asked Maria with a smile.

"No, that was Bill Lakeman." Bill was one of their best customers.

"It almost sounded like you were angry with him," said Terri.

Maria's eyes widened. "Gosh, I'm sorry," she said. "I didn't realize that's how I sounded. It's just that I'm so swamped. I have a dozen phone calls to return, a stack of orders to process, and several special projects to handle. I guess I don't feel like I have time to be nice."

Terri smiled sympathetically. "Take a deep breath, Maria. Don't worry about the backlog. This isn't an emergency room. Nobody's going to die if you don't handle a task immediately. Can someone else help you out?"

"Not really," Maria replied, shaking her head. "Everyone is backed up. To be honest, we're all feeling a lot of pressure lately."

"Thanks for letting me know," said Terri. "We certainly have to figure out how to take some of the pressure off you all so you can give our customers the best service possible."

"That's what we all really want to do," said Maria. "Thanks."

When Terri told Jud about her experience with Maria, he sighed.

"Let's call Lou Stafford," he said. "He's the expert on our advisory board in customer service."

One Minute Insights

☞ As an entrepreneur, the secret to success is generating CASH, CASH, CASH.

☞ Without good cash management, you'll never make it as an entrepreneur.

☞ Profit is the applause you get for taking care of your customers and creating a motivating environment for your people.

Creating Legendary Service

Lou Stafford was delighted that Jud and Terri had called. "Growing pains are a great problem to have," he said. "But taking care of your customers is not optional—it's imperative. Especially now as your company is growing, you've got to let your customers know that they are your number-one priority. Make them feel loved and respected. If you don't, pretty soon you won't have any customers. And without your customers, you don't have a company."

"But how do we do that well when there's so much work to do?" asked Terri.

"It's a question of focus," replied Lou. "You have to impress upon your people the importance of treating customers right. To keep customers today, you can't be content to merely satisfy them; you have to give them *legendary* service and create 'raving fans'—customers who are so excited about the way you treat them that they tell stories about you. In essence, they become part of your sales force."

"What do you mean by 'legendary service'?" asked Jud.

"I'll give you an example," said Lou. "My mother, when she was ninety, went to her refrigerator one day to get some ice. When she opened the ice section, water came pouring out; something clearly was wrong. Since she was an independent cuss and wanted to solve the problem herself, she went to the Yellow Pages. She called appliance-service companies, one after the other, only to be told that the earliest anyone could come out was in three weeks. Now, when you're ninety years old, three weeks is a long time!"

On the other end of the line, Jud and Terri chuckled.

"Discouraged, my mom was about to call me for help when she saw a little ad that said, 'Same-day service.' She called the number and soon a friendly voice was saying, 'We'd be happy to fix your refrigerator today, Mrs. Stafford. When would you like us to come?'

"'I have a choice?' my mom responded in amazement.

"'Absolutely.'

"'How about two o'clock?' Mom replied.

"Not only did a serviceman show up at two, but he had tools and was able to fix her refrigerator in short order. As he was leaving, he handed his business card to my amazed and happy mom. It had his home phone number on the back. 'Anytime, night or day, that you have a problem with your refrigerator, you can give me a call,' he said.

"What do you think my mother was doing for the next three days?" Lou asked. "She was calling everyone she knew about the great service she had received. She had become a raving fan."

"But how did this company pull off that kind of amazing service?" Terri asked.

"I wondered the same thing when my mother told me this story," replied Lou. "So I called the owner to find out how he could service people the day they called. It turned out that he had been a fix-it man in Massachusetts. Because of his health, his doctors suggested he move to a warmer climate. When he got to San Diego, he would find out when people were moving into a house they had just bought. He would then knock on the door and tell them that he was a fix-it man. If they needed any painting or repairs done, he would be happy to do it at a reasonable price. All he asked was that they agree to refer him to other customers if they liked his work.

"He always showed up on time, did what he said he would do with high quality, and charged a reasonable price. People loved his work. He built his business so successfully that eventually, when old customers would call, very often he didn't have time to help them because he was so busy. A number of people suggested to him that he start his own company. But he was reluctant because he was concerned about managing employees and having a big payroll."

"I can understand his reservations," said Jud with a laugh. "How did he resolve the situation?"

"He woke up in the middle of the night with a brilliant idea," Lou replied. "About 25 percent of the people living in San Diego are retirees. Many are bored. Most retirees could use some extra income. They'd love to have something to do, and help other people. So he put an ad in the local paper that said: 'Retirees: If you're good at fixing things, and you want to help people and make some extra money, give me a call.'

"It turns out he now has twenty-five to thirty retirees on call every single day. So when a customer like my mother calls, he has someone he can send out to her right away. And he carefully monitors the retirees' work, so that he only keeps the best and most reliable on his staff. Plus, he doesn't have the problem of a big payroll. If retirees don't work, they don't get paid. He told me with a laugh that in fact he had a hard time paying some of the people anyway, because it goofed up their Social Security. They just loved the work."

"Wow, what great, out-of-the-box thinking," said Terri.

"Sheldon Bowles, coauthor of *Raving Fans,* contends there are three secrets to creating raving fan customers: decide, discover, and deliver."

"What does he mean by 'decide'?" asked Terri as she jotted some notes.

"If you want to create raving fans, you don't just announce it; you have to plan for it," said Lou. "You have to decide what kind of experience you want your customers to have as they interact with every aspect of your organization."

"If we're putting customers first," said Terri, "shouldn't we ask them what kind of experience they want to have?"

"Yes and no," said Lou. "While you do want input from your customers, they often don't know what the possibilities are beyond their own experience. They don't have the big picture. That's why you and your key people have to decide first what kind of experience you want your customers to have."

"How do you do that, exactly?" asked Jud.

"One great idea came from Jan Carlzon, when he was president of SAS, the Scandinavian Airlines System. When he first joined the company, he traveled around Europe and met with all the employees to share his vision for the company. He said, 'We're not going to beat the competition because we have good airplanes. Having a good product or service is not your competitive edge.'"

"Why did he say that?" asked Jud.

"Because your competition can always copy your product or service," said Lou.

"But isn't having a good product or service important?" asked Terri.

"Absolutely," replied Lou. "But it's your entrée to doing business, not your competitive edge."

"Is a lower price your competitive edge?" asked Jud.

"No," said Lou. As Carlzon put it, 'We're not going to beat our competition because we have the lowest price. We don't want to get in a price war.' What you need is a fair price."

"So if it's not your product or service or price, what is your competitive edge?" asked Terri.

"As Carlzon put it, 'You're going to beat the competition on Moments of Truth,'" said Lou. "He defined a Moment of Truth as 'anytime a customer comes in contact with anybody in your organization in a way they can get an impression.'"

"Can you give an example of a Moment of Truth?" asked Terri.

"Sure," said Lou. "Let's take the example of a wake-up call in a hotel. What's the most common wake-up call in a hotel today?"

"I've been doing a lot of traveling lately," answered Jud, "so I can tell you. The phone rings, you pick it up, but there's no one there. Basically, a machine has called your room."

"Exactly," said Lou. "How about the second most common wake-up call?"

Terri said, "I've had wake-up calls where I get a recording that says something like, 'Good morning, this is your wake-up call.' But nobody's really on the line."

"It's true," said Jud. "Come to think of it, if you pick up the phone on a wake-up call and there is a human being on the other end, you hardly know what to say!"

"Exactly," said Lou. "Here's where my example of a Moment of Truth comes in. While I was staying at a Marriott in Orlando, the phone rang for my seven o'clock wake-up call. I picked it up and a woman said, 'Good morning, Mr. Stafford, this is Teresa. It's seven o'clock. It's going to be seventy-five degrees and beautiful in Orlando today, but your ticket says you're leaving. Where are you going?'

"I was taken aback," said Lou. "So I stammered, 'I'm going to New York City.'

"Teresa countered with 'Let me look at the *USA Today* weather map. Oh, no! It's going to be forty degrees and rainy in New York today. Can't you stay another day?'

"Now, where do you think I want to stay when I go to Orlando? I want to stay at the Marriott so I can talk to Teresa in the morning!" said Lou with a laugh.

"I get the picture," said Jud. "It's those little Moments of Truth that can make or break a customer relationship."

"Exactly," said Lou. "And for Carlzon and other great service providers, Moments of Truth cover every detail, right down to the coffee stains on the seats. When Donald Burr was chairman of People Express Airlines, he contended that if the flip-down trays were dirty, customers would assume that the planes' engines were not well maintained either. When looking for a place to stay after a long day's drive, how many people would choose a motel with a sign that's missing some lights?"

"Not me," said Terri.

"We've been talking about external customers. But it's important to recognize that everyone is a customer and everyone has a customer," Lou continued. "An external customer is someone outside your organization who does business with you. A person taking orders at a quick-service restaurant is a good example of someone serving external customers. An internal customer is someone within your organization who may or may not be serving external customers. For example, people who work in the human resources field have mainly internal customers. And some people, like those in the accounting department, have both external and internal customers. They send out bills and invoices to external customers and they provide reports and information for internal customers. The point is, everyone has a customer."

"So creating legendary service starts with an image of what kind of an experience you want your customers to have," Jud said. "And companies that provide great customer service analyze every Moment of Truth they have with customers, whether they are external or internal, and determine how they would like to have that experience played out."

"You've got it," said Lou.

"You mentioned that Sheldon Bowles's second secret was 'discover,'" said Terri, glancing at her notes. "What do you mean by that?"

"After you decide what you want to have happen, it's important to discover any suggestions your customers may have that will improve their experience with your organization. What would make their experience with you better? Ask them! But ask them in a way that stimulates an answer. For example, how many times have you been eating in a restaurant when the restaurant manager comes over and says to you, 'How was everything tonight?' Isn't your usual response, 'Fine'? That gives the restaurant manager no information. A more helpful conversation would begin with, 'Excuse me. I am the restaurant manager. I wonder if I could ask you one question. Is there anything that we could have done differently tonight that would have made your experience with us better?' That question invites an answer. If the customer says 'No,' you can follow it up with a sincere 'Are you sure?'"

"So what I'm hearing," said Jud, "is that if we want JTA to succeed in a big way, we're going to have to become masters of discovering what our customers are thinking."

"You don't have to read minds, but you do have to get creative about discovering what's on your customers' minds," Lou replied. "More often than not, this requires good listening skills."

"So an important part of creating raving fan service is a question of listening to customers and then taking action on what you hear," said Terri, summing up.

"Yes," said Lou, "with one condition: When a customer tells you something, you have to listen without being defensive. One reason people get uptight when they listen to customers is that they think they always have to do what the customer wants them to do. They don't understand that there are two parts to listening. Part one is, as Stephen Covey says, 'Seek first to understand.' In other words, listen for understanding. Try saying, 'That's interesting. Tell me more. Could you be more specific?'

"The second aspect of listening is deciding if you want to do anything about what you have heard," Lou continued. "That has to be separated from the understanding aspect of listening. And it is important to realize that deciding what to do does not have to take place right after you receive a suggestion. Do it later, when you have some time to think about it or talk it over with others. Realizing that you have time to think it over will make you less defensive and a better listener. First, listen to understand, and then decide what you want to do about what you have heard."

"I saw an example of defensive listening in the mall recently," Jud said. "I was walking behind a woman who had an eight- or nine-year-old son. As they walked past a sporting goods store, the kid looked over and saw a beautiful red bicycle outside the store. He stopped in his tracks and said to his mother, 'Boy, would I like a bike like that.' His mother nearly went crazy and started screaming: 'I can't believe it! I just got you a new bike for Christmas! Here it is March and you already want another one! I'm not going to get you another blankety-blank thing!' I thought she was going to nail the kid's head into the cement!"

"Sadly, that's a perfect example of someone who didn't listen for understanding before deciding," said Lou. "If she had said to the kid, 'Honey, what do you like about the bike?' he might have said, 'You see those streamers coming out of the handlebars? I really like them.' And those streamers could have been a cheap birthday present.

"Then, after listening to what he liked about the bike, the mother could have said, 'Honey, why do you think I can't get you that new bike?' The kid probably would have said, 'Because I just got a new bike for Christmas.'

"Listening without being defensive is also helpful if you make a mistake with a customer," continued Lou. "Defending what you have done will only irritate them. When they are upset, all customers want is to be heard. In fact, research has shown that if you listen to a customer complaint in a nondefensive, attentive way and then ask, 'Is there any way we could win back your loyalty?' eight out of ten times the customer will say, 'You have already done it. You listened to me.'"

"What if a customer makes a good suggestion or is upset about something that makes sense to change?" asked Terri.

"You can add that suggestion to your customer-service picture," replied Lou. "For example, recently I got a letter from a man who owns three McDonald's restaurants in the Midwest. The elderly customers from his restaurants suggested that during certain times of the day they should have tablecloths and candles on the tables, as well as staff taking their orders at the tables and delivering their food to them. After thinking about it, the owner realized that this was a pretty good idea. Now, between 4:00 and 5:30 in the afternoon—a prime meal-time for many of the elderly—the tables have tablecloths and candles, and the staff behind the counter come out and wait on the customers. The elderly pour into his restaurants during those hours.

"When you put together what you want your customers to experience with what they want to have happen, you will have a fairly complete picture of your desired customer-service experience," concluded Lou. "Listening to customers, fitting their needs into your framework, and then consistently improving your level of service will turn your customers into raving fans."

"You said something earlier about 'deliver,'" said Terri, again looking at her notes. "Can you explain that?"

"Sure," said Lou. "The concept is actually deliver plus 1 percent. Once you have a clear picture of the experience you want your customers to have—an experience that will satisfy them, delight them, and put smiles on their faces—you have to figure out how to get your people excited about delivering that experience *plus* a little bit more.

"The responsibility for establishing a customer-service vision rests with the owner or senior leadership. That's the visionary or strategic aspect of leadership, depending on the size of the company. When I say 'responsibility,' that does not mean that owners or management do not involve others, but the responsibility falls to the people at the top of the traditional hierarchy, whether you're running a mom-and-pop store or an international multiconglomerate. Once your desired customer-service experience is set and people are committed to it, the implementation—or operational aspect of leadership—begins.

"It is during implementation that most organizations get into trouble," Lou continued. "All the energy in the company moves up the hierarchy as people try to please and be responsive to their boss or bosses, instead of focusing their energy on meeting the needs of their customers. Bureaucracy rules, and policies and procedures carry the day. This leaves those who have contact with the customers unprepared and uncommitted. As a result, they quack like ducks."

"Ducks?" asked Terri.

"Yes," said Lou. "Wayne Dyer, the great personal-growth teacher, said years ago there are two kinds of people in life: ducks and eagles. Ducks act like victims and go 'Quack! Quack! Quack!' Too many of us act like ducks in life. Eagles, on the other hand, take initiative and soar above the crowd. As a customer, you can always identify a company that acts strictly by the rules when you have a problem and they confront you like quacking ducks: 'It's our policy. Quack! Quack! I didn't make the rules. Quack! Quack! I just work here. Quack! Quack! Do you want to talk to my supervisor? Quack! Quack! Quack!'

"I had a perfect example of this phenomenon when trying to rent a car recently," continued Lou. "I am a trustee at my alma mater. A while back, I was heading to a meeting in the small town where the school is located. I wanted to rent a car that I could drop off in the nearest city, Syracuse. Those who travel enough know if you drop off a car at a different place than where you rented it, the company charges a big drop-off fee. You can avoid that drop-off fee if you rent a car that came from where you are going. Knowing this, I asked the woman behind the counter, 'Do you have a Syracuse car?'

"She said, 'You're lucky. I happen to have one.' Then she went into the computer and prepared my contract.

"Now, I'm not a particularly detail-oriented person," said Lou with a laugh, "but as I was signing my contract, I saw a seventy-five-dollar drop-off fee out of the corner of my eye. I said, 'What's that seventy-five-dollar drop-off fee?'

"She said, 'I didn't add that. Quack! Quack!'

"I said, 'Who did?'

"She said, 'The computer. Quack! Quack!'

"I said, 'How do you tell the computer it was wrong?'

"She said, 'I don't know. Quack! Quack!'

"I said, 'Why don't you just cross it out?'

"She said, 'I can't. My boss will kill me. Quack! Quack!'

"'You mean I have to pay a seventy-five-dollar drop-off fee because you have a difficult boss?' I asked.

"She said, 'One time—Quack! Quack!—my boss let me cross it out.'

"'Why was that?'

"'The customer worked for the college here in town,' she said. 'Quack! Quack!'

"I said, 'That's great. I'm on the board of trustees there!'

"She asked, 'What does the board do? Quack! Quack!'

"I said, 'We can fire the president.'

"She said, 'What is your employee number? Quack! Quack!'

"'I don't have one,' I said.

"'What am I going to do? Quack! Quack!'

"It took me twenty minutes of psychological counseling to get out of this drop-off fee," Lou said. "I used to get angry with such people, but I don't anymore because I realize it's really not their fault.

"Who do you think this woman worked for, a duck or an eagle?" Lou asked.

"Obviously, a duck," replied Jud.

"That's right," said Lou. "If she worked for an eagle, she would have been given the leeway to solve the problem and keep her customer happy. In this case, the supervisor was the head mallard, because he or she simply quacked louder about the rules and regulations from a higher rung up the hierarchy. Who do you think the supervisory duck works for?"

"Another duck?" said Jud.

"Right," said Lou. "And who sits at the top of the organization? A great big duck. Have you ever been hit by eagle droppings? Obviously not, because eagles soar above the crowd. It's the ducks that make all the mess."

"How do you create an organization where ducks are busted and eagles can soar?" asked Jud.

"That's where I think you ought to talk to one of your board advisors for JTA, Nancy Kaline. As Nancy can tell you, the way to create eagles is to treat your people as partners so they feel empowered to act like they own the place. Nancy knows more about partnering with your people than anyone I've ever met."

"We'll do that, Lou," said Jud. "Thanks for all your help."

After their conversation with Lou, Jud and Terri shared all that they had learned about Moments of Truth with their entire staff. They asked people in each department to analyze all the touch points they had with their customers and to decide how they wanted those touch points to be played out. Later, they gathered together for a service-excellence day, to inspire one another with the results of their work.

One Minute Insights

☞ Look for Moments of Truth with your customers, to create the kind of experience you want them to have.

☞ Listen to your customers; discovering their ideas for improving the customer experience can make your company's vision and service even better.

☞ Don't create a company of ducks. Let your people soar like eagles to deliver superior customer service.

Helping People Soar Like Eagles

Nancy Kaline had taken over the presidency of her large, family-owned company from her father, who had built an incredible business from scratch with a classic "my way or the highway" leadership style. Yet that hadn't seemed to work in the last few years he ran the company.

"Several things changed," Nancy told Jud and Terri when they all got together. "First of all, business is much more complicated today than when my dad started out. Globalization, intense competition, and rapid and constant technological change were stretching him beyond his comfort zone. The one-man-band strategy of decision making just didn't cut it anymore as the company grew. Today's knowledge workers want a partnership relationship with their leaders."

"Partnership?" said Jud.

"Yes," said Nancy. "Dedicated employees today believe that ownership and management need them as much as they need the company. If they feel undervalued or uninvolved, they will go elsewhere. As with customers today, loyalty from your people has to be earned."

"How do you earn your people's loyalty?" Terri wondered aloud.

"By letting them bring their brains, not just their bodies, to work," said Nancy. "As Lou would say, let them soar like eagles instead of quack like ducks. To do that requires owners and bosses who are servant leaders."

"'Servant leadership?'" said Jud. "It sounds like the inmates are running the prison."

"Or some kind of religious movement," said Terri.

Nancy laughed. "To truly understand what servant leadership is all about, you have to recognize that there are two aspects to leadership: vision and implementation. The visionary aspect of leadership sets the direction, the values, and the major business initiatives. That's the 'lead' part of servant leadership. It's what I call strategic leadership. This is what my father was good at."

"Sounds like he was a big-picture guy," said Terri.

"He was," said Nancy with a smile. "And he had a number of experienced folks with him from the beginning, who would do anything to please him and make things happen. They were the typical employees of the past— loyal and willing to do what they were told. They dedicated themselves to the company in exchange for lifelong loyalty from their employer. Without folks like them, Dad would have been in trouble. He didn't focus much on implementation. He would set the direction and then expect that what he wanted to have happen, would happen."

"What do you mean?" asked Jud.

"He would tell people what the task was, and then he'd disappear," said Nancy. "He would head off looking for the next business opportunity. They were okay if they understood exactly what to do. But that wasn't always the case. Sometimes work didn't get done in a timely manner, and mistakes were made. When that happened, he would circle back and become a seagull manager, swooping in, making a lot of noise, dumping on everybody, and then flying out. But since my dad was loyal to them, they'd pick up the pieces and get back to work.

"When I took over, most of the original folks were retiring or heading out the door. It's a whole new ballgame now. People understand that good performance starts with clear goals, but what interests them the most is how those goals are going to be met—the operational leadership. That's where the 'servant' part of servant leadership comes in."

"Tell us more," said Terri.

"Today, people want managers who will work with them to accomplish goals. They want leaders who think of them as partners. That's what servant leaders do.

"And yet," said Nancy, "in most companies—whether large or small—leadership is commonly thought of in terms of a hierarchy, where the owner or president or CEO is in charge and everyone's energy is focused on pleasing their boss. That was happening with my father. In my experience, that kind of top-down leadership does not bring out the best in people."

"In other words," said Jud, "leadership that is perceived as side by side rather than top to bottom is more likely to create high performance and satisfaction."

"Right," said Nancy. "With such a side-by-side partnership, the focus is on helping people produce good results. When that happens, your folks feel good about themselves and the company wins."

Now Nancy really had Jud and Terri's attention.

"How can we as entrepreneurs make sure that we're emphasizing both performance and satisfaction?" asked Jud.

"By encouraging *everyone* to become a leader. Entrepreneurs who retain their people do just that. They realize that they can't do everything by themselves. They have to depend on the people they hire to take their dream, run with it, and make things happen. When mistakes are made, these leaders use these occasions as learning opportunities, rather than as a time to punish others."

"I see a lot of entrepreneurs who let their egos eat their brains," said Jud. "They start to think their business is all about them. They forget about the importance of their people. I hope I never fall into that trap."

"It's an easy trap to fall into," said Nancy. "If your organization is all about you, you don't allow your people to become committed to your dream. They'll shuffle in and out of your company, depending upon the offers they get elsewhere. When you think of your people as your partners, they'll begin to act like they own the place. They take responsibility for what they do. And that is exactly what you want them to do."

"How do you make people your partners, exactly?" asked Jud.

"You have to set up a strong performance management system," Nancy replied.

"The word 'system' often has a negative connotation," said Jud with a smile.

"You're right," said Nancy. "Most entrepreneurs don't think they need a system to manage their people. Yet as Peter Drucker often said, 'Nothing good happens by accident.' I am sure you have several people in your life who always remember your birthday."

They all nodded.

"They are very thoughtful people," continued Nancy. "How do you think they became so thoughtful? They are organized. They have some system that signals them several weeks before your birthday that it is coming up. That same kind of systematic thinking has to drive your management of people at work."

"What does a good performance management system involve?" asked Jud.

"There are three parts to an effective performance management system," said Nancy. "The first is performance planning. This is when you agree with your people about the goals and objectives that they should be focusing their energy on. All good performance starts with clear goals."

"So if people don't know where they are going, they have little chance of getting there," said Terri with a smile.

"That's for sure," said Nancy. "Too many people in organizations get punished for not doing what they didn't know they were supposed to do in the first place."

"And goal setting helps eliminate that," said Jud.

"It certainly helps," said Nancy. "Particularly if people not only know what they are being asked to do, but they also know what good performance looks like—what the performance standards are."

"Does the partnering begin with performance planning?" asked Terri.

"Yes," said Nancy. "But you have to remember that in performance planning, it's okay for the owner or manager to set the goals, because if there is a disagreement between a manager and a direct report about what the goals are, who wins?"

"The owner or manager, I assume," said Terri.

"Yes," replied Nancy. "Because that person represents the goals and objectives of the company. That doesn't mean that you don't involve your people in goal setting, particularly experienced people. It just means that the responsibility for goal setting rests with the manager. This is the 'lead' aspect of servant leadership."

"What's the second aspect of a good performance-review system?" asked Jud.

"*Day-to-day coaching,*" said Nancy. "This is where you invert the proverbial pyramid and turn the hierarchy upside down, so now you are essentially working for your people."

"Why do you do that?" asked Jud.

"Because then as a manager you become the cheer-leader and supporter of good performance by your people," said Nancy. "It's the role of managers to do everything they can do to help team members be success-ful. This is where the partnering relationship and the 'serve' aspect of servant leadership really kick in. You do everything you can to help team members soar like eagles."

"What's the third aspect of an effective performance management system?" asked Jud.

"Performance evaluation," said Nancy. "This is where managers and their direct reports sit down and ex-amine the performance of each team member over time."

"I used to dread performance-evaluation sessions," said Jud, "even though I knew Dirk, the CEO, was on my side."

"The reason most people dread their performance-evaluation sessions," said Nancy, "is they are never quite sure how they will be evaluated. They just hope they have a good relationship with their boss and, therefore, that their evaluation will go well."

"That certainly was the way it was with me," said Jud. "I remember Dirk had a form he had filled out on me."

"Oh, yes, the form," said Nancy. "When I go into most companies and organizations, people will say to me, 'You're going to love our new performance-evaluation form.' I always laugh, because I think that most of them can be thrown out."

"Why do you say that?" said Terri.

"Because these forms often measure things that nobody knows how to evaluate. For example, 'initiative' or 'willingness to take responsibility.' Or 'promotability'—that's a good one.

"When no one knows how to win on an evaluation form," continued Nancy, "they focus most of their energy up the hierarchy. After all, as Jud said, if you have a good relationship with your boss, you have a higher probability of getting a good evaluation."

"That really rings a bell with me," said Jud. "I never knew exactly how Dirk was going to evaluate me, except with my sales numbers, which were very specific."

"That gets back to performance standards, Jud," said Nancy. "Remember I said that all good performance starts with clear goals? You need performance standards. After all, if you can't measure something, you can't manage it. Often people are evaluated on unclear areas, where they don't even know what good performance looks like. And sometimes they haven't even been told that their boss is interested in a specific area."

"Let me get back to goal setting for a minute," said Terri. "Don't most organizations do a pretty good job on goal setting?"

"Yes, they do," replied Nancy. "But unfortunately, after setting goals, what do you think happens to those goals in most cases?"

Jud started to laugh. "I bet they get filed."

"You got it," said Nancy. "And no one looks at them until it's time for performance review."

"So the goals are not used actively during the year?" Terri said.

"No, they're not," replied Nancy.

"Why?" said Jud.

"Let me answer by asking you a question," said Nancy. "Of the three aspects of an effective performance management system, what's the one on which the least time is spent?"

"I know it's not performance evaluation," said Jud with a laugh, "because that seems to me to be the one aspect of what you're talking about that every manager focuses on."

"I bet it's day-to-day coaching," said Terri.

"Bingo!" said Nancy. "The least amount of time managers spend is on coaching. Yet this is the most important aspect of managing people's performance. It's here where feedback—praising progress and redirecting inappropriate behavior—moves to center stage. This is where your manager really becomes your partner, because he or she is giving you feedback on your goals and the results you are getting.

"If you want people to win and accomplish their goals, then they need somebody observing and monitoring their behavior after goals are established. This is when you guide them in the right direction if they are off base, and praise and cheer them on if they are on the money."

"This is really exciting stuff," said Jud.

"I'm glad you think so," said Nancy, "because it's absolutely key. To illustrate, let me share with you a story about a college professor I had. He was always in trouble with the university. He was investigated repeatedly by faculty committees. What drove the faculty crazy more than anything else was that at the beginning of every class he gave his students the final exam. When the faculty found out about that, they asked, 'What are you doing?'

"He'd say, 'I thought we were supposed to teach these students.'

"The faculty would say, 'You are, but you don't give the students the final exam ahead of time.'

"He'd say, 'Not only am I going to give them the final exam ahead of time—what do you think I am going to teach them throughout the semester? I'm going to teach them the answers, so that when they get to the final exam, they get As. You see, life is all about getting As, not some stupid normal distribution curve.'"

"What a great philosophy," said Jud.

"It is," said Nancy. "He impacted my leadership perspective significantly. Do you two go out and hire losers? Do you go around saying, 'We lost some of our losers last year, so let's go out and hire some new ones to fill those low slots'?"

"I sure hope we don't!" said Terri. "I'd like to think we go out and hire either winners or potential winners. Potential winners are people we think can be winners if they're coached in the right way."

"So you don't hire people to fit a normal distribution curve, do you?" said Nancy.

"Absolutely not," said Terri.

"So you want to be careful not to fall into that trap, whether officially or unofficially," continued Nancy. "So often managers think of their job as judging, evaluating, and criticizing their people. What it really is about is helping, cheerleading, and supporting their efforts."

"We hear you loud and clear," said Jud.

"Giving people the final exam ahead of time is equivalent to performance planning," continued Nancy. "Now they know exactly what's expected of them. Teaching people the answers is what day-to-day coaching is all about. If you see somebody doing something right, you give them an 'atta boy' or 'atta girl.' If they do something wrong, you just say, 'Wrong answer. What do you think would be the right answer?' In other words, you redirect them. And at the end of the performance period, giving people the same 'exam' you gave them at the beginning of the 'semester' makes the performance evaluation more effective."

"So you're saying there should be no surprises at an annual or semiannual performance evaluation," said Jud.

"That's exactly what I'm saying," said Nancy.

"Everyone should know what the test is going to be, and that they are going to get help throughout the year to achieve a high score. When you have a forced rating system where a certain percentage of your people have to lose, you lose everyone's trust. Now all they are concerned about is looking out for number one."

"I like your philosophy, Nancy," said Jud. "Are there any companies you've seen that are really using it?"

"Yes," said Nancy, "particularly with an enlightened top management. Garry Ridge, president of WD-40, has implemented 'Don't Mark My Paper—Help Me Get an A' as the major theme in his company. He is so emphatic about this and the performance management system that he fired the manager of a poor performer, rather than the employee himself, because that manager had done nothing to help the person get an A. He wants everyone to know that management is about a partnership relationship that helps people get As."

"What if you work closely with someone and they still don't deserve an A?" asked Terri.

"Then don't give it to them," said Nancy. "But recognize that they're probably in the wrong job. Now you move to career planning."

"So if we want our people to soar like eagles and take care of our customers, we have to create an environment where they can win—where they know that we're on their side—so they will be empowered to act like they own the place."

"That's it," said Nancy. "Leadership that emphasizes judgment, criticism, and evaluation of employees is a relic of the past. Effective leadership is about treating people the right way by providing the direction and encouragement they need to be their best. If you help your people get As, then you have a performance management system that will ignite them to blow your customers away. They feel good about themselves and want to return the favor to others."

"So it sounds like there's a real payoff for budding entrepreneurs," said Jud.

"There sure is," said Nancy. "If you treat your people right, they get passionate about their work and your company. Their passion overflows to your customers as they go out of the way to serve them well. Your customers feel that passion and experience great service, and end up being loyal to your company. Loyal customers tell stories about your company and are complimentary about your people. Your good reputation begins to spread like a prairie fire on a windy day! That remotivates your people. At the end of the day, passionate people and loyal customers bring success to your organization. The vision and strategic direction start it off, but how goals are accomplished and strategies are implemented is where the partnership relationship comes into play."

"We can't thank you enough," said Jud. "When it comes to taking care of our people, we've got plenty of great ideas to work on now."

One Minute Insights

☞ Working people today want a partnership relationship, not a top-down hierarchy.

☞ Everyone should be encouraged to be a leader.

☞ An effective performance management system helps people win rather than rating and berating them.

☞ The best management includes day-to-day coaching that catches people doing things right and redirects their efforts when they are off base.

☞ Work, as in life, is about getting As.

☞ Passionate people and loyal customers drive success in your organization.

Ego Issues

As the years passed, the company continued to grow. Terri remained as president for a number of years. But as the children got involved in school and extracurricular activities, it became obvious that Terri's ability to juggle the main responsibility for Alex and Elizabeth and overseeing the management of JTA was an overwhelming challenge.

"First things first," Jud and Terri told each other. "The kids are more important than the business," they agreed. So Terri decided to step down as president, and within a month JTA had a new president and chief operating officer, Forrest Oakes. Forrest had worked as a consultant with Jud and Terri in marketing their products and services, and had impressed them with his business acumen.

Linda—their first employee and still their opera-
tions manager—and several of their speaker affiliates
had reservations about Forrest. They felt he was a good
businessman, but that he just didn't share the values that
Jud and Terri had built the company on: ethical behavior
and mutually satisfying relationships. Rather than focusing first on doing things the right way and building respect
and trust with their people, customers, suppliers, and
community, Forrest's focus was mainly on their third-
ranked value: success. He was purely a "bottom line" guy.
Since Jud and Terri felt that business finance was not their
greatest strength, they thought this emphasis was needed
at JTA. As a result, they didn't listen to the concerns of
their people.

Despite the added expense of a new COO, the revenue brought in by the new businesses and the increase
in Jud's fees more than covered it. Forrest's focus was
clear—growth, growth, growth—and fate played into his
hands.

Jud was addressing a thousand business owners at a
conference in Dallas, and a *Wall Street Journal* writer was
sitting in his audience. After listening to Jud's inspired talk
"So You Want to Sell Something?," the journalist tracked
Jud down and interviewed him for an article. She asked
him how he'd become a professional speaker and grilled
him about his business philosophies.

When the article hit the stands, hundreds of phone calls came pouring in. It was clear from the overwhelmingly positive response that Jud's comments had struck a nerve. Jud's high profile in the press translated directly into increased business for JTA. Forrest cheered as requests for company training and materials doubled, then quadrupled. When the orders grew beyond JTA's ability to fulfill them, rather than panicking, Forrest charged on even harder.

Jud forgot Dirk's early career advice to stay humble. He became enamored with his own press and bought into Forrest's ego stroking. There was nothing Jud felt he couldn't do.

As a result, Jud was on the road all the time. He found it difficult to turn down any invitation to speak. He began to think every request for him to speak or conduct a training seminar was from someone who needed him, personally, and Forrest reinforced Jud's belief in his own importance. Forrest even demanded that clients pick up Jud in a limo.

While Jud was the main speaker in their organization, Forrest also creatively marketed their other speakers, as well as the learning materials JTA had developed. The company was on its way to becoming a business far greater than Jud and Terri's original dream.

When Jud wasn't on the road, he was in the office long hours, working side by side with Forrest to stimulate more business. It was only a matter of time before his ambitious president presented his ultimate business plan.

"Jud, you and JTA have become recognized leaders in the training and development business. We've gotten several attractive suitors that want us to roll up with some other companies in the industry and go public. The fact is, if we want to continue to grow, we need more capital. If we prepare to go public now, the sky is the limit. You and Terri will need a wheelbarrow to cart out all the money."

That image—plus the rush of adrenaline Jud felt when he thought of standing on the floor of the stock market on Wall Street the day their public offering was announced—drove Jud even more.

During the first years of their lives, Jud had been a model father to Alex and Elizabeth. He always seemed to have time to play with them, and he and Terri seemed like perfect parents. The fact that they balanced their family life with working together was an inspiration to others. But that all seemed to change when the *Wall Street Journal* article hit the streets and Forrest began feeding Jud's ego. Now life for Jud was all about work, work, work.

While Jud still loved Terri and the kids, he saw less and less of them. With Alex and Elizabeth both in school, it didn't take long for Jud to lose touch with their daily lives. A missed teacher meeting here, a soccer game there, sometimes even a birthday celebration that went unattended. Jud repeatedly made promises to take family vacations, most of which he felt the need to break.

In a feeble attempt to spend more time with Terri, Jud made a pact to set aside one date night per week. The pact soon became a joke. They fell months behind on their date calendar. Jud's broken promises and months of missed dates caused Terri to give up believing his promises. There was a "vacancy" sign hanging in his marital window, but Jud was oblivious to it.

It wasn't unusual for Jud to get most of his sleep on airplanes. In fact, during one especially grueling week of speaking engagements he spoke twice in Hawaii, sandwiched between engagements in San Francisco, Denver, and Boston. The trip generated a lot of revenue but left Jud exhausted. After coming home, he slept for twenty straight hours.

When Jud finally got up the next morning, Terri poured him a cup of coffee and begged him to slow down.

"This is our chance, Honey," he said. "We can have everything we ever wanted. We've got to make hay while the sun shines."

"Jud, I'm worried about you," Terri said. "You can't keep this up. And honestly, I'm tired of being a single parent. The kids hardly ever see you."

"I know, Sweetie, but now that our efforts are finally paying off, I can't risk letting opportunities slip through our fingers. Please be patient. Our time will come."

Terri not only was worried about Jud, she was also worried about JTA. Now that the kids were in junior high school, she was looking forward to getting more involved with the company again. But the place had changed. Her first clue to the state of the company came when Linda, their longtime employee, quit. Disturbed, Terri called her to find out why. When Linda tried to explain, she started to cry.

"I'll write you a letter," Linda said. "I'm just too upset to talk right now."

When the letter arrived, Terri sat and read it slowly:

Dear Terri,

I'm sorry I couldn't talk the other day, but I was an emotional wreck. I was part of Jud's and your dream from the beginning, and I am so sad that it seems to be dying.

Forrest is a madman. All he can think of is sales, sales, sales and growth, growth, growth, and he doesn't care how he achieves it.

Forrest has taken the heart right out of the staff. He doesn't care about anyone—only the numbers. And the saddest thing is, he's got Jud behaving the same way, too. The company just does not have the same values that we had when we started. I know change is inevitable, but I think JTA is heading for disaster with Forrest at the helm.

I know that this is hard for you to hear, Terri. But I love and respect you, and am sad beyond my ability to express myself to you.

Big hugs to Alex and Elizabeth. I hope you can win Jud back from Forrest.

Love to you,
Linda

When Terri confronted Jud with Linda's letter, Jud casually dismissed it.

"The company has just outgrown Linda," he claimed.

Terri couldn't believe it—she seemed to be living with a stranger. Jud had become obsessed by short-term results. Unfortunately, he had not yet learned that any strength taken to an extreme could become a liability. Terri had tried to get him to reach out to Tremendous or Red or any of their advisory board, but he kept avoiding them. Unbelievably, he didn't even answer Tremendous's phone calls.

The better the company did, the harder Jud worked. He considered every problem a personal challenge. With Forrest pushing him on, Jud became a man possessed.

One evening, he got home after nine o'clock. Terri was sitting alone in the kitchen.

He kissed her on the back of the neck and said, "Hi, baby, what's up?"

She sat still for a moment, then turned in her chair to look at him.

"Jud, I just got back from Elizabeth's dance recital. By myself. And earlier tonight I went to Alex's Boy Scout medal ceremony. By myself. Did you know that Alex twisted his ankle yesterday and can't play soccer this weekend? And that my sister had a suspicious mammogram this week? And oh, by the way, you missed our anniversary dinner last night. I enjoyed it thoroughly—alone!"

"Wait a minute, Honey—"

"You wait," she said, her voice quavering. "I've been waiting. And I'm tired of it. This is not the kind of life I signed up for. You need to make some serious choices soon, or someday you'll come home to an empty house." With that, Terri got up from the table, walked to the bedroom, and quietly closed the door.

Jud sat there, stunned. "Can this be happening?" he asked out loud.

Dirk's warning not to let your ego get out of hand came rushing back to him. Jud realized for the first time that he could win the battle—help the company go public—and lose the war—his family. It was hard to admit, but suddenly he realized that his life was completely out of balance. He was failing as a husband and father. With that realization came a blinding flash of the obvious: Success is not just about having a successful career. It's about having a great life.

When Jud crawled into bed that night, he gave Terri a hug and whispered into her ear, "I hear you loud and clear, Honey. I'll give Tremendous a call in the morning. I've gotten my priorities all goofed up."

* * *

"You sure have," Tremendous agreed after Jud told him the whole story. "Any man spending ten to twelve hours a day at the office—not to mention so much time on the road away from home and neglecting all of his other commitments—is on the wrong track. You've got to get more balance in your life."

Tremendous paused for emphasis. "Jud, you're running as fast as a racehorse and acting as stubborn as a mule. Unless you admit that the drive for money has you out of control, you will come home to an empty house someday. Spend more time with your wife and kids and pay attention to your health. Get some balance back in your life!"

"What would give me more balance?" asked Jud.

"Ruth Peale, Norman Vincent Peale's wife, wrote a great book years ago titled *Secrets of Staying in Love,*" replied Tremendous. "She argued that you can have it all in life as a married couple if you keep your priorities in order. First comes God, then your spouse, then your kids, and finally your job. The reason she put loving your spouse ahead of your kids is that she felt the best way you can show your kids you love them is to love their mother—or their father, as the case may be. Terri told me that after the kids were baptized, you became active in the church. You joined a men's support group and started to help teach a third-grade Sunday school class. What's happened to all that?"

"It all went out the window, I'm embarrassed to say," Jud replied. "I got too busy for God."

"Your dad forgave you after you got into trouble with Race Nelson, didn't he?"

"He sure did," said Jud, remembering his night in jail.

"Your heavenly father is the same way," said Tremendous with a smile in his voice. "He'd just like to be your first response rather than your last resort. I find it really helps if I take some time every morning to tell Him what I'm thankful for and share whatever's happening that day where I think I could use some help. When your ego gets in the way, you really Edge God Out."

"I hear you loud and clear," said Jud. "Do you have any thoughts about my relationship with Terri?"

"Sure do," said Tremendous. "Go home and tell Terri you've been a jerk and ask for her forgiveness. Then both of you give me a call."

* * *

"I know that you two have really been through a lot lately," said Tremendous, as Terri and Jud listened to him on the speakerphone, "and you're both very emotional. I don't have any silver bullets for you, but I do have some ideas for you to think about. Do you both love your kids?"

They said, "Of course we do, Tremendous."

"Then you have a powerful motivation to work things out. Remember, love is not an emotion, it's a decision. Jud, do you want your relationship with Terri to work?"

"Of course I do," said Jud.

"How about you, Terri?" asked Tremendous.

"I've had my moments lately," said Terri. "But yes, I do. Jud, I still see you as my husband and best friend."

"Okay, that's two yeses," said Tremendous. "Marriage counseling only works if both of you want it to work. So get yourself a good marriage counselor and commit to working at it until you think you're back on track with your marriage."

This time, Tremendous's seriousness overshadowed his joviality.

Jud and Terri sat in total silence for several moments. Slowly, their hands came together as Tremendous's words resonated with them. They agreed to get counseling and to begin working on their marriage with renewed energy and focus.

Jud admitted to Terri that the business, too, was out of balance and acknowledged that he had to do something about it, as well as his and Forrest's obsession with taking JTA public. He agreed to call Red O'Rourke and ask for help.

One Minute Insights

☞ Long-term success is about more than making tomorrow's numbers.

☞ Relationships at work and at home can deteriorate when they aren't nourished.

☞ A strength taken to an extreme can become a liability.

☞ Keep your priorities in order.

☞ Work to balance your business life with the rest of your life.

☞ Continually seek the wisdom of your mentors.

Turning Things Around

Jud reached Red on his first try.

"Before we get together," insisted Red after learning the nature of Jud's call, "you need to get an outside audit of JTA's books so we know where you are with cash. I know Juan Escobar would want that done. We both are uneasy about some of the things that Forrest Oakes has done."

Jud's relationship with Forrest became strained after he told him about the audit. Finances had never been Jud's strength or interest. He had turned that entire aspect of the business over to Forrest. Bringing in an outside group to look at the books put into question what Forrest had been doing, and Forrest didn't like it one bit. Jud's relationship with Forrest hit a low point when the audit was completed and Red suggested that the report be presented at an open meeting attended by Jud, Forrest, Terri, Juan, and Red himself.

The meeting to review the numbers began on a tense note. The financial results showed that Forrest had been reckless in his push toward going public. The company was carrying unacceptable levels of debt and revenues were no longer outpacing expenses.

After reviewing the numbers, Juan turned to Forrest. Forrest tried to look away, but Juan waited patiently to catch his attention. When Forrest looked up, Juan said, "If this were a public company and I was on your board of directors, I would ask for your resignation."

With that, Forrest lost it. He went into a tirade and started yelling at Jud and Terri about how tightfisted and shortsighted they were. Then he stormed from the room.

When Forrest was gone, Terri reached over and grabbed Jud's hand.

"I think what you've seen and heard here today leaves us with only one choice, Jud," said Terri. "Forrest has to go. We have to get back to basics."

That's exactly what they did. Red helped them develop a fair severance package for Forrest, and their advisory team devised a strategy for getting back on track.

The next day, Jud and Terri called an all-company meeting to announce the departure of Forrest. They were amazed at the positive energy from their people when they realized he was gone. It was obvious that Linda had been right about Forrest. Not only had he been mismanaging the finances, but he also had been wreaking havoc with their staff. The news that Forrest had left the company received a standing ovation.

Seeing everyone's commitment to turning JTA around, Jud and Terri made a special announcement.

"As some of you old-timers know, we had cash-flow problems when the company was just starting out. At that time, many of you helped us turn the company around. Just as we did back then, we're going to create task forces to see how we can increase our sales and cut our costs. But this time—when we right the ship and our finances are back in good shape—we want to take everyone to Hawaii to celebrate."

"You certainly couldn't do that if you were a public company," said Tremendous with a laugh when Jud and Terri told him about their plan later. "Imagine explaining to your stockholders a celebration to Hawaii. Once you go public, it's hard to have that kind of freedom to do what you think might be best for your people—especially when it costs a fistful of money."

"We now realize that," said Jud.

"Going public is a smart move for some companies when they need additional capital to expand and build the business. But it may not be appropriate for a personal-services business like yours. Do you want my priceless advice rather than my good advice?" asked Tremendous.

"Yes, we want your priceless advice," Terri said with a smile.

"Actually, I'm going to give you both. My good advice is: Don't ever ask anyone for their advice. When you ask for their advice, you're asking them to tell you what to do. You don't want a mandate. Now here's my priceless advice: Ask people for their counsel. That way you're gathering information so you can make your own well-informed decision."

"Okay, we want your counsel, Tremendous," said Jud.

"Then I would recommend that you get this idea of going public out of your head, Jud. And Terri, you get back involved in the business and grow it gradually over time. JTA can give you everything you ever wanted from a business. Plus, it will give you the time to have a balanced life. Rabbi Kushner, the author of *When Bad Things Happen to Good People,* once told me that during all his years as a rabbi, he never heard anyone on their deathbed say, 'I wish I had gone to the office more.' The people he spoke with all wished they had spent more time with people they loved."

"Good point," said Jud. "Any other thoughts?"

"Yes," said Tremendous. "Try substituting strategic patience for crisis management. You're on the right track now. Just keep doing the right things, one day at a time."

Jud and Terri thanked Tremendous for his priceless advice. They jointly agreed to drop the idea of going public and committed to growing the company gradually over time. They realized that they not only needed to stay on top of their finances, but they needed to take ongoing care of their customers and restore the faith and trust of their people as well. They developed a schedule for staying in touch with Red and Juan about the company's finances, and with Lou and Nancy about their customers and people.

In a major positive development, Jud and Terri had the inspired idea to ask Jeremy Britton to join them as their general manager. He was an old buddy of Jud's— they had played football together in high school—and had been the best man at their wedding. Terri had always admired and trusted Jeremy. He was cautious and reliable, yet curious and adaptable when it was appropriate. He had been a successful manager in both the hospitality and health-care fields, and Jud and Terri felt he would be a perfect match for their culture. They knew that Jeremy's problem-solving ability would set them on the right track.

Before Jeremy agreed to join Jud and Terri, he took some vacation time to come to JTA, interview all the employees, and get a sense of the challenges that might lie ahead. Afterward, he sat down with Jud and Terri to discuss his findings.

"As I'm sure you both know, the company has two major problems," Jeremy told Jud and Terri. "First, cash reserves are low and debt levels are high. That needs to get turned around. Second, morale took a hit under Forrest Oakes, and you'll need to do some work to repair the damage. Fortunately, you have a steady revenue stream and some good strategies in place to begin solving these problems."

"We have a long way to go," admitted Jud.

"But you've made a good start," said Jeremy with a smile. "Your people are excited that you're taking back the leadership."

"But we still face some real challenges," said Jud.

"Are you up to the challenge of helping us, Jeremy?" asked Terri.

"I'm fascinated by your business—I know you're offering the kind of sales and personal-growth insights that can help a lot of people in their lives and careers. And I think you've got great people. I can't think of anyone I'd rather work with than you two," said Jeremy.

With that, Jud, Terri, and Jeremy hugged.

One Minute Insights

☞ It's better to patiently implement a solid business strategy than to recklessly push for growth.

☞ The wrong leader can send you off in directions you don't want to go.

☞ The right leader at the right time can help steer things in the right direction.

Putting It All Together

Jud and Terri, with yeoman help from Jeremy, spent the next several years putting into action all they had learned from Red and Juan about finances, as well as Lou and Nancy's advice about delivering legendary service and helping their people soar like eagles. The results surpassed their highest hopes.

Jeremy did a great job of implementing the recommendations from the task forces organized by Jud and Terri. He constantly reinforced the need for everyone in the organization to know how important it was for sales to exceed expenses and to reduce accounts receivable. But he also realized that you can't cost-cut your way to prosperity. He emphasized that while everyone had to use good judgment and stay on top of the finances, they also needed to focus on sales.

Jeremy pressed everyone, not just salespeople, to ramp up their efforts to pursue new opportunities that could lead to increased revenue. What impressed everyone was that Jeremy served as a good role model.

Jeremy found a new revenue stream when he contacted a college friend, Matt Rhoads, who had become the CEO of LJF Corporation, one of the nation's largest food-service companies. Matt was doing an excellent job running the company, but he realized that to stay competitive, LJF would have to become more innovative. Seeing a mutually beneficial opportunity, Jeremy worked closely with Matt to spearhead the formation of "LJF University."

The university's curriculum, taught on the company's intranet, focused on intrepreneurship. The curriculum was designed to inspire LJF employees to take ownership of new initiatives and get others to buy in. Essentially, it was a way of promoting innovative, entrepreneurial thinking in a corporate environment. The curriculum was based on the following principles:

1. Companies must constantly innovate. Without innovation they tend to do what they've always done and run the risk of getting stale and becoming competitively disadvantaged.

2. For a company to thrive, it must tap the individual initiative of its team members. This must be a major area of focus.

3. On any initiative being pursued, team-member buy-in is absolutely essential for success.

4. If a company wants its people to be intrepreneurial in their thinking, they must be kept well informed about the company's processes and visions— and the impact of these processes and visions on profit and loss.

5. Leaders must give team members everything they need to be self-motivated and take initiative to succeed.

6. Companies must reward the creativity of their people.

7. If a team member owns an initiative, he or she should be accountable for all aspects of its success.

8. Companies must encourage resourcefulness and out-of-the-box thinking.

9. All thought leaders must be constantly focused on customer needs and how to satisfy and exceed them.

10. Leaders and managers must work to maximize team-member involvement in all key initiatives to tap the collective intellect of the team.

When Jeremy presented the guidelines to Matt at LJF, he encouraged him to put together a company task force of four or five forward-thinking managers who could dig deeper into each point to make sure it would be a good fit for LJF.

"Anytime you can give key people opportunities for authorship, they will buy in with greater resolve and determination," Jeremy said.

The game plan worked. The food-service company became innovative and started growing by leaps and bounds. Matt Rhoads attributed the enhanced revenues and profits to the initiative JTA had formulated for them and the close working relationship he had developed with Jeremy Britton. As a result, JTA also grew—a lot.

To keep results and relationships in balance, JTA developed an "I CARE" legendary service initiative:

Ideal service
Culture of service
Attentiveness
Responsiveness
Empowerment

The I CARE initiative started when every department at JTA recommitted to identifying their Moments of Truth with customers and delivering their ideal customer-service vision.

To foster a culture of service that increased attentiveness and responsiveness from everyone, Jud, Terri, and Jeremy decided to eliminate the Employee of the Month Program, which had been part of the JTA culture for years. In its place they substituted an Employee of the Moment Program. Anytime someone was seen— by either an external or an internal customer—as going beyond the call of duty to serve that customer, there was an immediate celebration. An eagle's nest was established where associates, armed with cameras, were ready to photograph eagles in flight. A Wall of Fame was created where stories and pictures of JTA associates caught creating raving fan customers were displayed. There were no restrictions on how many times a person could appear on the Wall of Fame.

To help people soar like eagles, the JTA performance management system was transformed into a partnering-for-performance system. Every manager was taught coaching essentials so they could establish clear goals and performance standards, praise progress, and redirect efforts that were off the mark. Managing by Wandering Around became a way of life. In addition, managers were expected to have one-on-one meetings with each of their direct reports every two weeks. These meetings lasted only fifteen to thirty minutes, but they permitted direct reports to update their managers on their progress and ask for any additional help that might be needed. This kept both members of the partnership—manager and direct report—up to date.

As a result, when it came to performance reviews, there was no new news. These end-of-year discussions were really a review of all the things that the partners—managers and their direct reports—had been talking about all year long. The goal of every partnership was to empower people to be problem solvers, not subordinates waiting for superiors to tell them what to do.

All these efforts took several years to implement. They produced not only great financial results but a work environment that was the envy of other companies. When Jud and Terri looked at the year-end numbers, they had the same thought.

"Remember three years ago when we said we'd take everyone to Hawaii after we pulled out of the financial hole we were in?" said Jud. "I think the time has come."

"I agree!" said Terri.

Jeremy agreed as well, and the plans were set. The following February, all of the JTA associates headed to Maui for a four-day celebration of the company's turn-around. On the last evening, a local band was hired to play at a farewell luau. Everyone danced barefoot in the sand. At the end of the evening, the leader of the band was so blown away by the energy of the group that he looked down from the stage and said, "I don't know what you guys do for a living, but keep it up. You've got to be doing something right!"

With JTA back on its feet, Jud and Terri turned some of their energy to their own finances. This was a response to some priceless advice from Tremendous.

"Now that you have stopped the bleeding at JTA, it's a good time to begin focusing on your own financial dreams," said Tremendous. "During the financial crisis you just went through, you learned how important good banking relationships are."

"We sure did," said Jud. "The turnaround has helped us sleep better, because all our money was tied up in the company."

"One of the things that saved you both was that you didn't suffer from the 'I need' disease that afflicts so many people," said Tremendous. "They buy too much lifestyle, and then their net worth shows minimal growth. You have to watch your 'lifestyle costs.'"

"What's the best way to do that?" asked Terri.

"Planning," said Tremendous. "The best advice Gloria and I ever heard occurred early in our marriage. Our pastor advised us to put 10 percent of our income into a savings account every month and then give another 10 percent away to charities and other nonprofit organizations. He told us that if we learned how to live on 70 to 80 percent of our income, we'd be wealthy someday."

"So you believe in tithing?" asked Jud.

"I certainly do," said Tremendous. "I once heard Sir John Templeton, one of the great financial investors of our time, speak. He told everyone that the best financial advice he'd ever given anyone was to tithe. He argued that you should not wait until you have all kinds of money before you tithe. Make it a monthly habit, no matter how low your income is.

"Templeton said he's never known anyone who had tithed at least 10 percent of their income for ten years," continued Tremendous, "who didn't have what they gave away coming back to them tenfold. When you reach out to help others, you invariably get more back in return."

"Do you have any real-world examples of that?" asked Jud.

"Yes. Paul J. Meyer, a well-known entrepreneur and author, and his wife, Jane, immediately come to mind. They tithe about 70 percent of the money they take in. This wasn't always so. After determining how much money they thought they would need the rest of their lives—plus what they wanted to give to their kids and grandkids—they committed to giving any excess away to good causes. They started out with about 15 to 20 percent, but now it's almost 70 percent because of all the money that's been coming back in over and above their needs."

"That's fascinating," said Terri.

"Truett Cathy is another example of this," said Tremendous. "He's the founder of Chick-fil-A. One time I heard him say in a speech that he wished the Lord hadn't made this replenishment promise, because the more he gives away, the more comes back—and now he has even more responsibilities managing his sizable charitable organization."

"Is giving money away what you're recommending?" asked Jud.

"It's your decision," said Tremendous with a smile. "Remember, this is priceless advice. But this has to do with the last thing I learned from Sheldon Bowles."

"I remember Sheldon encouraged entrepreneurs to *play to your passion* as well as find people who will *pay for your passion*. If you don't do what you love, you'll never work hard enough to be the best," said Jud. "And if no one will pay you to do what you love, you have a hobby, not a business."

"And don't forget *plus your passion*."

"Yes," said Jud. "You have to find ways to create new income streams that build off what you are already passionate about."

"You certainly have done a good job on those things, individually and with your organization," said Tremendous. "You have a lot of people who love what they do and are getting paid to do it. And you have been creative and resourceful in finding new ways to earn income that are an outgrowth of your speaking business."

"Thanks," said Jud with a smile. "Now stop stalling. What's the last thing you learned from Sheldon?"

"It's what we've been talking about: Pass on the prosperity from your passion. That's what Sheldon calls the test of perpetual prosperity—that you'll never really be successful unless you help others. Helping others does not just involve the financial gains from your prosperity, but also includes sharing your time and talent. Mentoring others is a way to pass on what you've gotten from others along the way."

This conversation made Jud feel he had come full circle. From being a broke kid out of college with lots of ambition, he had become a successful entrepreneur. Yet in some ways he was still unfulfilled. It made him think about the fragility of life and the more important issues, like leaving a legacy that could positively impact others.

Noticing the thoughtful look on Jud's face, Tremendous said, "What's on your mind?"

"I was thinking about what kind of legacy Terri and I can leave."

"Interesting you should mention that," said Tremendous. "Bob Buford, in his book *Halftime,* argues that at some point in all of our lives we want to move from success to significance—from getting to giving. I think that's what a legacy is all about."

"That's certainly where Terri and I are right now," said Jud.

"Everyone leaves a legacy," said Tremendous, "whether they intend to or not. People who are more intentional about it usually leave a better legacy behind. Everything you are and possess today, good or bad, will pass down to those who come after you—not only the monetary stuff, but also your beliefs and philosophy. The legacy you leave is the legacy you live."

"How can Terri and I be more intentional about the legacy we leave?" asked Jud.

"You have to learn what real prosperity is," said Tremendous. "Riches aren't a fixed pie that gets divided up with only so much to go around. The pie grows constantly by supplying goods and services to others. In the process, you either add value to whatever is already there or you create something new. As you help others realize their potential, you may well be turning a horse and buggy into a jet plane! The result is a much bigger pie, and some of the slices will probably come back to you. As I mentioned earlier, when you reach out to help someone else, you often get more back in return. It's about nurturing a spirit of abundance rather than scarcity."

That conversation with Tremendous focused Jud and Terri on giving back to others. It played out in their company in two ways. First, they started a gain-sharing program: They took 10 percent of their profit every year and shared it equally with all of their people. Every month the balance sheet was shared, so everyone knew how well they were doing and what it would take to increase everyone's share of the pie.

They also took another 10 percent of their profit and gave it back to employees to tithe to charity causes of their own choosing. The only requirements were that the charity have 501(c) tax status and that they did not give to the general fund, but rather to a specific project. This made sure people really became involved in their charity.

They also started JTA for Others, a nonprofit group that people could contribute to with monthly paycheck deductions and various fund-raising activities. The charities that JTA for Others focused on were chosen by the employees. The donations went to a wide range of worthy causes, including hurricane relief, environmental preservation, aid to the needy, medical care for those in financial crisis, and travel funds for associates who needed to be with faraway loved ones who were sick, injured, or in trouble in some way.

The head of HR was given an "angel fund" to disperse among associates when circumstances deemed it necessary. Jud would leave global voice-mail messages when somebody was hurting and ask for love and prayers to be sent their way. JTA truly became a family organization—and in more ways than one.

One Minute Insights

☞ To live a happy and fulfilled life, be generous with your wealth, time, and talent.

☞ Giving can be much more rewarding than receiving.

☞ We all leave legacies. Be intentional about making a positive difference with yours.

☞ You can't predict the good that can come from helping or forgiving someone.

Building a Legacy

Jud and Terri found that Tremendous was right. When you give to others, it comes back to you in spades. JTA continued to grow and thrive over the years. It was chosen as one of the best companies to work for, and in the process attracted the attention of Jud and Terri's grown children, Alex and Elizabeth. By this time, they both had graduated from college and were out in the workforce. Alex had attended a hotel school and was working in the hospitality industry. Elizabeth, who had always been a fashion plate, was working in the retail apparel industry.

When Jud and Terri, who were now more committed to each other and in love than ever before, realized that their kids might be interested in joining their company, they decided to form a family council. It would include the two of them, Alex and Elizabeth, and Jeremy, who had become like a family member and was now the president and COO of the company. They hired a consultant, Jim Elder, who had been working with family businesses for more than twenty years, to meet with them for a minimum of one day a quarter.

When Jim Elder began working with the family, he interviewed each of the five members of the family council. He came to Terri and Jud last.

"I'm going to ask you the toughest question that the founders of a family business have to answer. Do you want Alex, Elizabeth, and Jeremy to be owners of the company, regardless of whether they ever work in it?"

"Why do you ask that?" said Jud.

"Because it's one of the biggest problems I encounter with family businesses. Family members and close friends take on positions in the organization that they are not qualified to hold, just to protect their ownership. Ownership and management position should be two separate things. If Jeremy, Alex, and Elizabeth become owners, they should be paid the benefits of ownership regardless of their involvement in the company. If Alex and Elizabeth decide to take management positions, they should be paid a fair-market salary for that responsibility, over and above any ownership shares. This tends to focus everybody's energy on how they can best contribute to the success of the organization. No matter what they do, even if they are not involved in running the company at all, their ownership is protected."

That's exactly what Jud and Terri decided to do. In the beginning, they gradually turned over 19.5 percent ownership each to Alex and Elizabeth and 10 percent to Jeremy. Over time, as everyone realized what a long-term partner Jeremy was, the kids came to Jud and Terri and argued for equal status for Jeremy. Eventually, all five members of the family council owned 20 percent of the company.

Alex turned out to be a chip off the old man's block and became a great speaker and cheerleader himself. Elizabeth, like her mom, was better suited for the operational side, and she soon became head of sales.

Years later, Jud and Terri quietly celebrated their fortieth anniversary by indulging in one of their favorite pastimes: babysitting their grandson, Kevin. They spent the evening sitting in their armchairs in front of the fireplace while Kevin played with building blocks on the rug at their feet. Reflecting back on the last forty years, they talked about how far their entrepreneurial adventure had come.

"We're so blessed," said Jud. "But our success would never have been possible without all of the mentors who played such key roles in our lives."

"You're right," said Terri.

"Remember my old high school buddy, Race Nelson? When I think about it, I have him to thank for my life taking a positive turn," said Jud with a laugh. "When I got caught in Race's car with marijuana, I thought it was the end of the world. Now I'm grateful it happened, because I learned so much from that. It changed my life. In a way, Race was my first mentor."

"I'd vote for Dirk Gardner," said Terri. "After all, he launched your speaking and sales career."

"He sure did," said Jud. "But the best mentor of all has been the ever-available, ever-generous, ever-endearing Charlie 'Tremendous' Jones, who brought us together. He always seems to have the right advice at the right time."

They continued to reminisce about the people who changed their entrepreneurial lives the most. They agreed they'd never forget Tremendous's friend Harris Palmer, who gave them the fundamental advice that came to guide every one of their business decisions:

- Sales have to exceed expenses.
- Collect your bills.
- Take care of your customers.
- Take care of your people.

They felt fortunate that Red O'Rourke and Juan Escobar understood the importance of CASH, CASH, CASH. They remembered how Lou Stafford had taught them that legendary service was a choice that started with Moments of Truth and continued with their I CARE initiative. They talked about the importance of Nancy Kaline's insights that your people are not your subordinates, they are your partners, and that you can't expect people to take care of your customers if you don't create an environment where they can bring their brains to work, act like owners, and soar like eagles.

As they reviewed all that they had learned, Jud and Terri committed to continued mentoring of Alex and Elizabeth, as well as to reaching out and helping other young people who had the courage to take advantage of the free-enterprise system that was the foundation of the global economy. They shared a passion to encourage those who were willing to step out and take the risk to become entrepreneurs.

"It's not always easy," said Jud, "and it's important for people to know that being an entrepreneur is about committing to success one step at a time."

"Yes, indeed," said Terri. "Tremendous was right when he told us we had to substitute strategic patience for crisis management."

"He sure was," said Jud. "He said we were doing all the right things. We just needed to keep doing them, one day at a time."

"Some days it felt more like one minute at a time!" Terri recalled with a laugh.

"That's for sure," said Jud. "But Rome wasn't built in a day, and neither is a successful business."

"Or a successful marriage, for that matter," Terri added wryly.

Jud let out a laugh, got up from his chair, and gave his wife a kiss. Their grandson looked up at them and let out a shriek. In the few minutes they'd been talking, he had stacked up a formidable pile of blocks.

"Look," said Terri, pointing to her grandson's creation. "He's already got the hang of this building thing."

"Give him another twenty years and he might very well be an entrepreneur, building his own successful company," said Jud proudly.

Terri smiled at her grandson. "Good job, Kevin. You just keep building, one minute at a time, one block at a time!"

Appendix

 **Top 20 Attributes of Successful Entrepreneurs**

Listed below are the top 20 attributes of a successful entrepreneur that were featured in this book:

1. *Resourceful*
2. *Purposeful*
3. *Focused*
4. *Risk-taking*
5. *Problem-solving*
6. *Salesmanship-oriented*
7. *Visionary*
8. *Optimistic*
9. *Leadership-oriented*
10. *Ambitious*
11. *Innovative*
12. *Integrity-based*
13. *Adaptable*
14. *Communicative*
15. *Self-motivated*
16. *Strategic*
17. *Team-oriented*
18. *Determined*
19. *Curious*
20. *Balanced*

Go to www.estrengths.com to take a free assessment and see how you measure up in each key attribute.

Acknowledgments

A book like this doesn't get written by the authors alone. Mentors like Charlie "Tremendous" Jones and Sheldon Bowles come into your life to help impact your thinking. That certainly is what Ethan Willis did for us with his entrepreneurial strengths questionnaire and passion to develop successful entrepreneurs.

We have continued to learn wonderful insights about life and work from great speakers and authors like Ken McFarland, Bill Gove, Zig Ziglar, Peter Drucker, Cavett Robert, Brian Tracy, Stephen Covey, Harvey Mackay, Patrick Lencioni, Wayne Dyer, Jim Collins, Jim Rohn, Mark Sanborn, Suze Orman, Tom Peters, Tom Landry, Phil Hodges, Rabbi Harold Kushner, and Jan Carlzon.

Ken would never be where he is today if it weren't for the mentoring he got from Paul Hersey. Their relationship goes back to the sixties, when they were teaching at Ohio University, and continues today as they collaborate and cooperatively compete with each other's entrepreneurial companies in Escondido, California. Ken also thanks Norman and Ruth Peale for their inspiration and the positive effect it has had on his life.

Ken thanks Drea Zigarmi, Scott Blanchard, and Vicki Essary for their research on the relationship among leadership, employee passion, customer devotion, and organizational vitality.

Thanks also to Randy Garn from Prosper, Inc., and Tom McKee and Kevin Small from The Ken Blanchard

Companies, who encouraged us to write this book. Without their gentle shove, this manuscript might never have come to fruition. Kevin was also instrumental in bringing us together with the fine folks at Random House/Doubleday, Michael Palgon and Roger Scholl.

Without expert writers better than us, we would have been lost, particularly Martha Lawrence, Ken's writing partner and inspiration. Susan Drake, Jonellen Heckler, and Dr. Terry Paulson, colleagues of Don's, gave invaluable editorial assistance.

Special thanks also go to people who read the manuscript and were willing to give us feedback. They include Kemmons Wilson Jr., Jerry Britton, Beverly Britton, Joe Hensley, Ruth Ann Hensley, L. D. Beard, Sondra Fondren, Mark Ruleman, Frank Colvett Sr., Earl Blankenship, Frank Watson Jr., Dr. Paul Green, David Waddell, Scott Messmore, Joan Messmore, Greg Casals, Phil Donovan, Steve Williford, Bentley Goodwin, Chris Mercer, Jerry Cardwell, Petie Parker, Pat Kandel, Carmela Southers, Jan Nast-Carter, Martha Maher, Linda Hulst, Gwin Scott Jr., Terri Murphy, and all the good people from Skaneateles Country Club.

Ken and Margie Blanchard are indebted to a number of entrepreneurs who went out of their way to help them during the infant stages of The Ken Blanchard Companies. They include Dick Pratt, entrepreneur extraordinaire who heads up the largest company in Australia, and who was the first to give them the four keys to being a successful entrepreneur. Red Scott from San Diego emphasized the importance of CASH, CASH, CASH. Advice from John Anderson from Illinois, Peter Meinig from Oklahoma, John Metz from Pennsylvania, Alan Raffee from California, and Dick Reiten from Oregon—who formed the original advisory board for their company—was invaluable as Ken and Margie launched their entrepreneurial career. John Eldred, a fabulous consultant to family businesses, came into their lives at the right time and helped integrate their son Scott, daughter Debbie, and Margie's brother Tom McKee into their business. Special thanks are also due to the advisory board of The Ken Blanchard Companies: Pat Hyndman, Bob Lorber, Tom Muccio, Garry Ridge, and Richard Whiteley.

Don acknowledges the late Dick Gardner, his early mentor and insightful manager, who gave him his first job out of college.

Special thanks to Richard Andrews for all his help on our contracts, which has permitted this book to become a reality. Special thanks also go to four organizations that have impacted us both: the Young Presidents' Organization (YPO), the National Speakers Association (NSA), Toastmasters International, and the Entrepreneurs' Organization (EO). All four of these organizations are full of cheerleaders and encouragers for people who want to make a difference in the world.

Last but not least, thanks to our wives, Margie and Terri, who permitted us to marry above ourselves and become better human beings in the process. They are important entrepreneurial partners for us today.

Selected Readings

By Ken Blanchard

The One Minute Manager (with Spencer Johnson)

Leadership and the One Minute Manager (with Drea Zigarmi and Pat Zigarmi)

The One Minute Manager Builds High Performing Teams (with Don Carew and Eunice Parisi-Carew)

Self Leadership and the One Minute Manager (with Susan Fowler and Laurence Hawkins)

The Generosity Factor (with Truett Cathy)

Know Can Do! (with Paul J. Meyer and Dick Ruhe)

Leading at a Higher Level (with the Founding Associates and Consulting Partners of The Ken Blanchard Companies)

Whale Done! (with Jim Ballard, Chuck Tompkins, and Thad Lacinak)

By Don Hutson

The Sale

The Contented Achiever (with Chris Crouch and George Lucas)

Speaking Secrets of the Masters (with the members of Speakers Roundtable)

Insights into Excellence (with the members of Speakers Roundtable)

Taking Charge: Lessons in Leadership (anthology)

By Sheldon Bowles

Raving Fans (with Ken Blanchard)

Gung Ho! (with Ken Blanchard)

High Five! (with Ken Blanchard)

Big Bucks! (with Ken Blanchard)

Kingdomality (with Richard Silvano and Susan Silvano)

By Charlie "Tremendous" Jones

Life Is Tremendous

The Price of Leadership

Four-Star Leadership for Leaders

Finding Freedom in Forgiveness

From a Father's Heart

Humor Is Tremendous

By Michael Gerber

The E-Myth

The E-Myth Revisited

E-Myth Mastery

Awakening the Entrepreneur Within

Services Available

Ken Blanchard and Don Hutson speak to conventions and organizations throughout the world. They have content available in audio CD and DVD formats, as well as Internet-based training.

The Ken Blanchard Companies conduct seminars and in-depth consulting in the areas of customer service, leadership, team building, performance management, and quality. Don's firm, U.S. Learning, specializes in sales growth, relationship enhancement, management, and entrepreneurship.

For further information on Dr. Ken Blanchard's activities and programs, contact:

The Ken Blanchard Companies
125 State Place
Escondido, CA 92029
www.kenblanchard.com
1-800-728-6000, from the United States
1-760-489-5005, from anywhere

To find out more about Don Hutson addressing your meeting or working with your company, please contact:

Don Hutson, CPAE, CEO
U.S. Learning, Inc.
516 Tennessee Street, 2nd Floor
Memphis, TN 38103
Don@DonHutson.com
www.DonHutson.com
1-800-647-9166 or 1-901-767-0000

About Prosper

Ethan Willis is founder of Prosper, Inc., a recognized global leader in distance education for entrepreneurs. Founded in 1999, Prosper has helped more than 40,000 students discover and then leverage their entrepreneurial strengths to build successful businesses.

Prosper believes your education should pay. Their one-on-one coaching methods deliver accelerated results in the following areas:

- Entrepreneurship
- Small business
- e-commerce and Internet marketing
- Real estate investing
- Online stock market investing
- Personal finance

To learn more about Prosper's one-on-one coaching, call 1-866-704-4028, or visit their Web site at www.prospering.com.

About the Authors

Ken Blanchard has had an extraordinary impact on the day-to-day management of millions of people and companies. He is the author of several bestselling books, including the blockbuster international bestseller *The One Minute Manager*® and the giant business bestsellers *Leadership and the One Minute Manager, Raving Fans,* and *Gung Ho!* His books have combined sales of more than 18 million copies in more than twenty-five languages. In 2005, Ken was inducted into Amazon's Hall of Fame as one of the top twenty-five bestselling authors of all time.

Ken is the chief spiritual officer of The Ken Blanchard Companies, an international management training and consulting firm. He is also cofounder of the Lead Like Jesus Ministries, a nonprofit organization dedicated to inspiring and equipping people to be servant leaders in the marketplace. The College of Business at Grand Canyon University bears his name.

Don Hutson of Memphis, Tennessee, is CEO of U.S. Learning. He has given more than five thousand speeches in twenty-two countries in the past thirty-five years and is in the National Speakers Association's Speakers Hall of Fame. Don was on the founding board of the National Speakers Association, served as its third president, and received the Cavett Award as Member of the Year. He is on the board of directors of the Society of Entrepreneurs and served as its president.

Don Hutson is author or coauthor of nine books, including *The Sale* and *The Contented Achiever,* and has published his sales and management training programs on CD and DVD. He is featured regularly on both PBS and TSTN Television.

Ethan Willis of South Pasadena, California, is co-founder and CEO of Prosper, Inc., a leader in one-on-one coaching, with courses in entrepreneurship, e-commerce, Internet marketing, real estate investing, personal finance, and stock market investing.

Ethan has made a significant contribution to the distance-education industry by training more than 150,000 entrepreneurs in seventy-six countries. He was named a 2005 Ernst and Young Entrepreneur of the Year and a 2006 NRCC Business Man of the Year.

Ethan has owned and operated more than a dozen businesses, including Education Success, Inc., Money Mentor Center, Prosper Media, and AdCafe.

Discover ~~Your~~ Strengths
Free Entrepreneur Strengths Assessment

It's Time...

...to discover your strengths and unlock your full potential. This book was written to help people discover their entrepreneurial strengths, and discusses 20 key attributes of successful entrepreneurs. A measure of each of these attributes can be found in every successful entrepreneur.

Take a look at yourself—you will find some of these traits as well. Which ones do you possess, and to what extent? Which ones are you lacking, and what can you do to incorporate those you are lacking into your arsenal?

We have helped Fortune 500 companies experience breakthroughs that led them to even greater levels of success. Now, we want to help you experience personal breakthroughs! Let us help you:

- Discover your true strengths and talents
- Strengthen your leadership abilities
- Boost your confidence
- Align your individual goals and competencies
- Start on the path to living the life of your dreams

Discover Your Strengths
Free Entrepreneur Strengths Assessment

The System

We have created an assessment—a system—that will help you leverage the attributes you possess. It will also help you make changes that will allow you to develop the other attributes.

Our team has developed a FREE entrepreneurial attributes survey. This survey will reveal your entrepreneurial strengths and weaknesses, allow you to tap into your strong areas, and help you grow and strengthen your weaknesses.

The assessment consists of a series of questions designed to identify your areas of competency and areas you should seek to improve. Once you complete the assessment, you will have instant access to a personal assessment report of your entrepreneurial attributes.

You can access this free assessment at www.estrengths.com. This assessment will inspire you to achieve even greater success in your life. Visit the site, take the survey, and start on your path to greatness!

www.estrengths.com

Home Study Kit

Reinvent Your Life for Fun and Money

100%
Downloadable
Includes audio,
video, and ebooks.

Entrepreneurship Is Transforming America...

All great success stories start with an idea. Are you one idea away from the success of your dreams? Do you need help coming up with or executing your idea? The One Minute Entrepreneur Home Study Kit has the tools you need to make your idea work.

From this comprehensive digital program, you'll learn Ken Blanchard's proven, powerful, and extremely profitable system for discovering, developing, and unleashing powerful business ideas. You'll discover how to launch your new business, find sources of funding, and take care of your customers and your team. Best of all, you will learn how to make your dream a reality.

Are you ready to get started? Visit www.omehomestudy.com to order your One Minute Entrepreneur Home Study Kit and begin your journey.

www.omehomestudy.com

Virtual Conference
Hear It Straight from the Author

Exclusive Opportunity for Entrepreneurs

We want to help you create your own personal success story. We don't care about your past failures, your personality, or your situation. Together, we can eliminate anything that may be holding you back—and turn your ideas into action! It's time to build on your strengths and make your business a reality.

We have created an exclusive virtual conference featuring Ken Blanchard for those who believe they have the potential to leverage their strengths and achieve their dreams!

In this virtual conference, Ken discusses the motivation and driving factors behind writing this book and summarizes key points that will make a dramatic difference to you in your journey, including the four actions you must take to be successful:

- Assure that sales exceed expenses
- Collect your bills
- Take care of your customers
- Take care of your people

Additionally, Ken discusses the 20 attributes of successful entrepreneurs—and how they apply to you. This virtual conference gives rare insight into the minds of successful entrepreneurs, and is an exclusive opportunity to experience the magic of Ken Blanchard.

Taking action is essential for anyone to find, increase, and enjoy success. Act on Ken's personal invitation to attend the virtual conference by visiting:

www.omeconference.com